ABOUT THIS WORKBOOK

This workbook was designed to facilitate English Language Learners (ELLs) in their language development. The importance of practice and application is the foundation for this resource. It is important that English Language Learners are given the guidance, support, and opportunities to practice language learning in familiar and academic context.

The workbook activities coincide with the California English Language Development Standards. Educators can track and record their students' progression and acquisition of the English language.

Guided activities provide both educators and ELLs with appropriate levels of support. The activities expose the students to the format and language expectations of the English Language Proficiency Assessment for California (ELPAC). Similar to a test prep manual, this workbook will help familiarize ELLs with the ELPAC. However, this workbook can be a great resource to ALL language learners and doesn't have to be limited to just EL students.

The practice activities are another added layer of support for ELLs. The expected outcome of English language acquisition can be complemented with this great resource!

THE CURIOUS MIND EDUCATOR | ENGLISH LANGUAGE DEVELOPMENT

OTHER ELPAC RESOURCES AVAILABLE:

KINDERGARTEN
SPEAKING

LISTENING

READING

WRITING

FIRST GRADE
SPEAKING

LISTENING

READING

WRITING

SECOND GRADE
SPEAKING

LISTENING

READING

WRITING

THIRD-FIFTH GRADE
SPEAKING

LISTENING

READING

Table of Contents

Writing

Describe a Picture

Write About an Experience

Write About Academic Information

Justify an Opinion

THIS PAGE INTENTIONALLY LEFT BLANK

Writing
Describe a Picture

This section includes:
- Guided Activities
- Teacher's ELD Standards Record Sheet
- Student Practice Activities:
  - Writing practice for a picture

Alignment to CA ELD Standards:

Part I: Interacting in Meaningful Ways
A.2 Exchanging Information and Ideas
Exchanging information and ideas with others through oral collaborative discussions on a range of social and academic topics

Part II: Learning About How English Works
B.3 Expanding and Enriching Ideas
Using verbs and verb phrases

Part II: Learning About How English Works
B.4 Expanding and Enriching Ideas
Using nouns and noun phrases

Part II: Learning About How English Works
B.5 Expanding and Enriching Ideas
Modifying to add details

Part II: Learning About How English Works
C.6 Connecting and Condensing Ideas
Connecting ideas

Part II: Learning About How English Works
C.7 Connecting and Condensing Ideas
Condensing ideas

Alignment to CCSS:

SL.3.1, 6; L.3.1, 3, 6
SL.4.1, 6; L.4.1, 3, 6
SL.5.1, 6; L.5.1, 3, 6

W.3.5; SL.3.6; L.3.1, 3, 6
W.4.5; SL.4.6; L.4.1, 3, 6
W.5.5; SL.5.6; L.5.1, 3, 6

W.3.5; SL.3.6; L.3.1, 3, 6
W.4.5; SL.4.6; L.4.1, 3, 6
W.5.5; SL.5.6; L.5.1, 3, 6

W.3.5; SL.3.4, 6; L.3.1, 3, 6
W.4.5; SL.4.4, 6; L.4.1, 3, 6
W.5.5; SL.5.4, 6; L.5.1, 3, 6

W.3.1-3, 5; SL.3.4, 6; L.3.1, 3, 6
W.4.1-3, 5; SL.4.4, 6; L.4.1, 3, 6
W.5.1–3, 5; SL.5.4, 6; L.5.1, 3, 6

W.3.1-3, 5; SL.3.4, 6; L.3.1, 3, 6
W.4.1-3, 5; SL.4.4, 6; L.4.1, 3, 6
W.5.1–3, 5; SL.5.4, 6; L.5.1, 3, 6

Writing
Describe a Picture

Guided Activities Direction:

1. Show students the picture and the short paragraph that is presented as if written by a peer.
2. Follow the teacher directions.
3. **Say** the **Teacher Script** (indicated by (**SAY**))
4. Guide students through:
   - Editing and correcting errors in the sentences
   - Adding more details to the sentences
   - Using complete sentences
   - Connecting and condensing ideas
   - Expressing something that might happen next
5. Questions are indicated by 1
6. Then have students practice with additional writing activities.

Note: The Summative Assessment includes two questions, but four questions are provided here for practice.

Guided Activity #1

Name:

> **SAY** You and your partner need to describe a picture. Your partner has started writing a paragraph. The paragraph may contain errors. Read your partner's paragraph below and then follow the directions.

> The kids are playing. The little girl is stack block high up. The boy is on the rug. The boy is playing with cars.

---

1   Look at this sentence.

The kids are playing.

Rewrite this sentence with more details.

_____

_____

_____

_____

_____

_____

Guided Activity #1 - cont'd

2 Look at this sentence.

The little girl is stack block high up.

The sentence has TWO errors. Rewrite the sentence correctly.

_____

_____

_____

_____

_____

3 Look at these two sentences.

The boy is on the rug. The boy is playing with cars.

Combine the two sentences into one.

_____

_____

_____

_____

_____

4 Write a new sentence to describe what the other little girl is doing.

_____

_____

_____

_____

_____

Guided Activity #2

Name:

SAY **You and your partner need to describe a picture. Your partner has started writing a paragraph. The paragraph may contain errors. Read your partner's paragraph below and then follow the directions.**

The student is learning. The teacher is careful poured the mixture. The student is writing. The student is writing in the notebook.

---

1 Look at this sentence.

The student is learning.

Rewrite this sentence with more details.

_____

_____

_____

_____

_____

Guided Activity #2 - cont'd

2 Look at this sentence.

The teacher is careful poured the mixture.

The sentence has TWO errors. Rewrite the sentence correctly.

_____

_____

_____

_____

_____

_____

3 Look at these two sentences.

The student is writing. The student is writing in the notebook.

Combine the two sentences into one.

_____

_____

_____

_____

_____

4 Write a new sentence to describe something else you see in the picture.

_____

_____

_____

_____

Guided Activity #3

Name:

SAY You and your partner need to describe a picture. Your partner has started writing a paragraph. The paragraph may contain errors. Read your partner's paragraph below and then follow the directions.

The girls are studying. The girl is write a letter four school. Her sister is reading. It is a book about history.

---

1 Look at this sentence.

The girls are studying.

Rewrite this sentence with more details.

_____

_____

_____

_____

_____

Guided Activity #3 - cont'd

2 Look at this sentence.

The girl is write a letter four school.

The sentence has TWO errors. Rewrite the sentence correctly.

_____

_____

_____

_____

_____

3 Look at these two sentences.

Her sister is reading. It is a book about history.

Combine the two sentences into one.

_____

_____

_____

_____

_____

4 Write a new sentence to describe where you think the girls are.

_____

_____

_____

_____

_____

Guided Activity #4

Name:

SAY You and your partner need to describe a picture. Your partner has started writing a paragraph. The paragraph may contain errors. Read your partner's paragraph below and then follow the directions.

They are taking turns practicing. The ball flyed when the boy kicking it. His friend cheered. He cheered when the ball went in.

---

1 Look at this sentence.

They are taking turns practicing.

Rewrite this sentence with more details.

_____

_____

_____

_____

_____

Guided Activity #4 - cont'd

2 Look at this sentence.

The ball flyed when the boy kicking it.

The sentence has TWO errors. Rewrite the sentence correctly.

_____

_____

_____

_____

_____

3 Look at these two sentences.

His friend cheered. He cheered when the ball went in.

Combine the two sentences into one.

_____

_____

_____

_____

4 Write a new sentence to describe what the the students will do next.

_____

_____

_____

_____

Guided Activity #5

Name:

(SAY) **You and your partner need to describe a picture. Your partner has started writing a paragraph. The paragraph may contain errors. Read your partner's paragraph below and then follow the directions.**

Students are waiting in line. The boy getted the first books. The girl is next. She is waiting patiently.

---

1 Look at this sentence.

Students are waiting in line.

Rewrite this sentence with more details.

_____

_____

_____

_____

_____

Guided Activity #5 - cont'd

2 Look at this sentence.

The boy getted the first books.

The sentence has TWO errors. Rewrite the sentence correctly.

_____

_____

_____

_____

_____

3 Look at these two sentences.

The girl is next. She is waiting patiently.

Combine the two sentences into one.

_____

_____

_____

_____

_____

4 Write a new sentence to describe what will happen after the boy receives his book.

_____

_____

_____

_____

Writing: *Describe a Picture*

ELD Standards Record Sheet

Directions:

1. Look at the CA ELD standards (**BELOW**) that correspond to this section.
2. Reference these specific standards for the template Record Sheet.
3. Use the following template Record Sheet to monitor students' proficiency levels for the **GUIDED ACTIVITIES** in this section.
4. Fill out all the information. Circle, check, highlight the proficiency level. (*There is space for 20 students. Make additional copies, as needed*)
5. Retain for your records to be used during grading, parent/student conferences, lesson planning, ELD documentation, etc.

Suggestion: You can make one copy of each guided activity and/or the student practice sheets and laminate them. Organize the laminated sheets onto a book ring. Now it'll be easily accessible for whole group, small group, one-on-one, centers, etc. Copy as many of the ELD Standards Record Sheet as you need and keep it handy along with the activities.

Writing: *Describe a Picture*

ELD Standards Record Sheet

CA ELD Standards & Proficiency Levels

Part I: Interacting in Meaningful Ways
A.2 Interacting via Written English

EMERGING (EM)	EXPANDING (EX)	BRIDGING (BR)
Requires **Substantial** Support	Requires **Moderate** Support	Requires **Light** Support
GRADE 3		
• Collaborate with peers • Joint writing projects of short informational/literary texts • Technology use when applicable (i.e. publishing, graphics, etc.)	• Collaborate with peers • Joint writing projects of longer informational/literary texts • Technology use when applicable (i.e. publishing, graphics, etc.)	• Collaborate with peers • Joint writing projects of a variety of longer informational/literary texts • Technology use when applicable (i.e. publishing, graphics, etc.)
GRADE 4		
• Collaborate with peers • Joint writing projects of short informational/literary texts • Technology use when applicable (i.e. publishing, graphics, etc.)	• Collaborate with peers • Joint writing projects of longer informational/literary texts • Technology use when applicable (i.e. publishing, graphics, etc.)	• Collaborate with peers • Joint writing projects of a variety of longer informational/literary texts • Technology use when applicable (i.e. publishing, graphics, etc.)
GRADE 5		
• Collaborate with peers • Joint writing projects of short informational/literary texts • Technology use when applicable (i.e. publishing, graphics, etc.)	• Collaborate with peers • Joint writing projects of longer informational/literary texts • Technology use when applicable (i.e. publishing, graphics, etc.)	• Collaborate with peers • Joint writing projects of a variety of longer informational/literary texts • Technology use when applicable (i.e. publishing, graphics, etc.)

ELD Standards Record Sheet

CA ELD Standards & Proficiency Levels

Part II: Learning About How English Works
B.3 Using Verbs and Verb Phrases

EMERGING (EM)	EXPANDING (EX)	BRIDGING (BR)
*Requires **Substantial** Support*	*Requires **Moderate** Support*	*Requires **Light** Support*
GRADE 3		
• *Use frequently used verbs* • *Use different verb types (e.g. doing, saying, being/having, thinking/feeling)* • *Use different verb tenses (e.g. simple past for recounting an experience)* • *Appropriate for the text type and discipline to convey time*	• *Use a <u>growing number</u> of verb types (e.g. doing, saying, being/having, thinking/feeling)* • *Use a <u>growing number</u> of verb tenses (e.g. simple past for retelling, simple present for a science description)* • *Appropriate for the text type and discipline to convey time*	• *Use a <u>variety</u> of verb types (e.g. doing, saying, being/having, thinking/feeling)* • *Use a <u>variety</u> of verb tenses (e.g. simple present for a science description, simple future to predict)* • *Appropriate for the text type and discipline to convey time*
GRADE 4		
• *Use various verbs* • *Use various verb types (e.g. doing, saying, being/having, thinking/feeling)* • *Use various verb tenses (e.g. simple past for recounting an experience)* • *Appropriate for the text type and discipline for familiar topics*	• *Use various verbs* • *Use various verb types (e.g. doing, saying, being/having, thinking/feeling)* • *Use various verb tenses (e.g. simple past for retelling, timeless present for science explanation)* • *Appropriate for the <u>task</u>, text type and discipline* • *<u>For an increasing variety of familiar and new topics</u>*	• *Use various verb* • *Use various verb types (e.g. doing, saying, being/having, thinking/feeling)* • *Use various verb tenses(e.g. timeless present for science explanation, mixture of past and present for historical information report)* • *Appropriate for the task and text type* • *For a <u>variety</u> of familiar and new topics*
GRADE 5		
• *Use frequently used verbs (e.g. take, like, eat)* • *Use various verb types (e.g. doing, saying, being/having, thinking/feeling)* • *Use various verb tenses (e.g. simple past for recounting an experience)* • *Appropriate for the text type and discipline for familiar topics*	• *Use <u>various</u> verb types (e.g. doing, saying, being/having, thinking/feeling)* • *Use various verb tenses (e.g. simple past for retelling, timeless present for science a description)* • *Appropriate for the <u>task</u>, text type and discipline* • *<u>For an increasing variety of topics</u>*	• *Use various verb types (e.g. doing, saying, being/having, thinking/feeling)* • *Use various verb tenses (e.g. timeless present for science description, mixture of past and present for narrative or history explanation)* • *Appropriate for the task and text type* • *For a <u>variety</u> of topics*

ELD Standards Record Sheet

CA ELD Standards & Proficiency Levels

Part II: Learning About How English Works
B.4 Using Nouns and Noun Phrases

EMERGING (EM)	EXPANDING (EX)	BRIDGING (BR)
Requires **Substantial** Support	Requires **Moderate** Support	Requires **Light** Support
GRADE 3		
• *Expand noun phrases in simple ways in order to enrich:* 　◦ *The meaning of sentences* 　◦ *Add details about ideas, people, things, etc. (e.g. adding an adjective to a noun)*	• *Expand noun phrases in a <u>growing number</u> of ways in order to enrich:* 　◦ *The meaning of sentences* 　◦ *Add details about ideas, people, things, etc. (e.g. adding comparative/superlative adjectives to nouns)*	• *Expand noun phrases in a <u>variety</u> of ways in order to enrich:* 　◦ *The meaning of sentences and* 　◦ *Add details about ideas, people, things, etc. (e.g. adding comparative/superlative adjectives to nouns, simple clause embedding)*
GRADE 4		
• *Expand noun phrases in simple ways in order to enrich:* 　◦ *The meaning of sentences* 　◦ *Add details about ideas, people, things, etc. (e.g. adding an adjective)*	• *Expand noun phrases in a <u>variety</u> of ways in order to enrich:* 　◦ *The meaning of sentences* 　◦ *Add details about ideas, people, things, etc. (e.g. adding adjectives to noun phrases or simple clause embedding)*	• *Expand noun phrases in an <u>increasing variety</u> of ways in order to enrich:* 　◦ *The meaning of sentences and* 　◦ *Add details about ideas, people, things, etc. (e.g. adding general academic adjectives and adverbs to noun phrases or more complex clause embedding)*
GRADE 5		
• *Expand noun phrases in simple ways in order to enrich:* 　◦ *The meaning of sentences* 　◦ *Add details about ideas, people, things, etc. (e.g. adding an adjective to a noun)*	• *Expand noun phrases in a <u>variety</u> of ways in order to enrich:* 　◦ *The meaning of sentences* 　◦ *Add details about ideas, people, things, etc. (e.g. adding comparative/superlative adjectives to noun phrases or simple clause embedding)*	• *Expand noun phrases in an <u>increasing variety</u> of ways in order to enrich:* 　◦ *The meaning of sentences* 　◦ *Add details about ideas, people, things, etc. (e.g. adding comparative/superlative and general academic adjectives to noun phrases or more complex clause embedding)*

ELD Standards Record Sheet

CA ELD Standards & Proficiency Levels

Part II: Learning About How English Works
B.5 Modifying to Add Details

EMERGING (EM) →	EXPANDING (EX) →	BRIDGING (BR)
*Requires **Substantial** Support*	*Requires **Moderate** Support*	*Requires **Light** Support*
GRADE 3		
• *Expand sentences with adverbials (e.g. adverbs, adverb phrases, prepositional phrases)* • *Use these to provide details about a familiar activity or process (e.g. time, manner, place, cause) (e.g. They walked to the soccer field.)*	• *Expand sentences with adverbials (e.g. adverbs, adverb phrases, prepositional phrases)* • *Use these to provide details about a familiar or <u>new activity</u> or process (e.g. time, manner, place, cause) (e.g. They worked quietly; They ran across the soccer field.)*	• *Expand sentences with adverbials (e.g. adverbs, adverb phrases, prepositional phrases)* • *Use these to provide details about a <u>range</u> of familiar and new activities or processes.(e.g. time, manner, place, cause) (e.g. They worked quietly all night in their room.)*
GRADE 4		
• *Expand sentences with familiar adverbials (e.g. basic prepositional phrases)* • *Use these to provide details about a familiar activity or process (e.g. time, manner, place, cause) (e.g. They walked to the soccer field.)*	• *Expand sentences with a <u>growing variety</u> of adverbials (e.g. adverbs, prepositional phrases)* • *Use these to provide details about a familiar or <u>new activity</u> or process (e.g. time, manner, place, cause) (e.g. They worked quietly; They ran across the soccer field.)*	• *Expand sentences with a <u>variety</u> of adverbials (e.g. adverbs, adverb phrases, prepositional phrases)* • *Use these to provide details about a <u>variety</u> of familiar and new activities or processes.(e.g. time, manner, place, cause) (e.g. They worked quietly all night in their room.)*
GRADE 5		
• *Expand and enrich sentences with adverbials (e.g. adverbs, adverb phrases, prepositional phrases)* • *Use these to provide details about a familiar activity or process (e.g. time, manner, place, cause)*	• *Expand and enrich sentences with adverbials (e.g. adverbs, adverb phrases, prepositional phrases)* • *Use these to provide details about a familiar or <u>new activity</u> or process (e.g. time, manner, place, cause)*	• *Expand and enrich sentences with adverbials (e.g. adverbs, adverb phrases, prepositional phrases)* • *Use these to provide details about a <u>variety</u> of familiar and new activities or processes.(e.g. time, manner, place, cause)*

ELD Standards Record Sheet

CA ELD Standards & Proficiency Levels
Part II: Learning About How English Works
C.6 Connecting Ideas

EMERGING (EM)	EXPANDING (EX)	BRIDGING (BR)
Requires **Substantial** Support	Requires **Moderate** Support	Requires **Light** Support
GRADE 3		

• Combine clauses in a few basic ways
• To make connections between and to join ideas (e.g. creating compound sentences using and, but, so)
	• Combine clauses in an <u>increasing variety</u> of ways (e.g. creating compound and complex sentences)
	• to make connections between and to join ideas, for example:
	  ○ <u>to express cause/effect (e.g. The deer ran because the mountain lion came.)</u>
	  ○ <u>to make a concession (e.g. She studied all night even though she wasn't feeling well.)</u>
		• Combine clauses in a <u>wide variety</u> of ways (e.g. creating compound and complex sentences)
		• to make connections between and to join ideas, for example:
		  ○ to express cause/effect (e.g. The deer ran because the mountain lion approached them.)
		  ○ to make a concession(e.g. She studied all night even though she wasn't feeling well.)
		  ○ <u>to link two ideas that happen at the same time (e.g. The cubs played while their mother hunted.)</u>

GRADE 4		

• Combine clauses in a few basic ways
• To make connections between and to join ideas in sentences (e.g. creating compound sentences using coordinate conjunctions, such as and, but, so)
	• Combine clauses in an <u>increasing variety</u> of ways (e.g. creating complex sentences using familiar subordinate conjunctions)
	• to make connections between and to join ideas in sentences, for example:
	  ○ <u>to express cause/effect (e.g. The deer ran because the mountain lion came.)</u>
	  ○ <u>to make a concession (e.g. She studied all night even though she wasn't feeling well.)</u>
		• Combine clauses in a <u>wide variety</u> of ways (e.g. creating complex sentences using a variety of subordinate conjunctions)
		• to make connections between and to join ideas, for example:
		  ○ to express cause/effect (e.g. Since the lion was at the waterhole, the deer ran away.)
		  ○ to make a concession
		  ○ <u>to link two ideas that happen at the same time (e.g. The cubs played while their mother hunted.)</u>

GRADE 5		

• Combine clauses in a few basic ways
• To make connections between and to join ideas
• To provide evidence to support ideas or opinions (e.g. You must X because X.) (e.g. creating compound sentences using and, but, so)
	• Combine clauses in an <u>increasing variety</u> of ways (e.g. creating compound and complex sentences)
	• to make connections between and to join ideas, for example:
	  ○ <u>to express cause/effect (e.g. The deer ran because the mountain lion came.)</u>
	  ○ <u>to make a concession(e.g. She studied all night even though she wasn't feeling well.)</u>
	• To provide reasons to support ideas (e.g. X is an extremely good book because X)
		• Combine clauses in a <u>wide variety</u> of ways (e.g. creating compound and complex sentences)
		• to make connections between and to join ideas, for example:
		  ○ to express cause/effect (e.g. The deer ran because the mountain lion approached them.)
		  ○ to make a concession (e.g. She studied all night even though she wasn't feeling well.)
		  ○ <u>to link two ideas that happen at the same time (e.g. The cubs played while their mother hunted.)</u>
		• To provide reasons to support ideas (e.g The author persuades the reader by X.)

ELD Standards Record Sheet

CA ELD Standards & Proficiency Levels

Part II: Learning About How English Works
C.7 Condensing Ideas

EMERGING (EM)	EXPANDING (EX)	BRIDGING (BR)
Requires **Substantial** Support	Requires **Moderate** Support	Requires **Light** Support
	GRADE 3	
• Condense clauses in simple ways to create precise and detailed sentences (e.g. It's green. It's red. It's green and red.)	• Condense clauses in a <u>growing number</u> of ways to create precise and detailed sentences (e.g. through embedded clauses as in, It's a plant. It's found in the rainforest. It's a green and red plant that's found in the tropical rainforest.)	• Condense clauses in a <u>variety of ways</u> to create precise and detailed sentences (e.g. through embedded clauses and other condensing, as in, It's a plant. It's green and red. It's found in the tropical rainforest. It's a green and red plant that's found in the tropical rainforest.)
	GRADE 4	
• Condense clauses in simple ways to create precise and detailed sentences (e.g through simple embedded clauses as in, The woman is a doctor. She helps children. The woman is a doctor who helps children.)	• Condense clauses in an <u>increasing variety of ways</u> to create precise and detailed sentences (e.g. through a growing number of embedded clauses and other condensing as in, The dog ate quickly. The dog choked. The dog ate so quickly that it choked.)	• Condense clauses in a <u>variety of ways</u> to create precise and detailed sentences (e.g. through various types of embedded clauses and other ways of condensing, as in, There was a Gold Rush. It began in the 1850s. It brought a lot of people to California. The Gold Rush that began in the 1850s brought a lot of people to California.)
	GRADE 5	
• Condense clauses in simple ways to create precise and detailed sentences (e.g through simple embedded clauses as in, The book is on the desk. The book is mine. The book that is on the desk is mine.)	• Condense clauses in an <u>increasing variety of ways</u> to create precise and detailed sentences (e.g. through a growing number of types of embedded clauses and other condensing as in, The book is mine. The book is about science. The book is on the desk. The science book that's on the desk is mine.)	• Condense clauses in a <u>variety of ways</u> to create precise and detailed sentences (e.g. through various types of embedded clauses and some nominalizations, as in, They were a very strong army. They had a lot of enemies. They crushed their enemies because they were strong. Their strength helped them crush their numerous enemies.)

Writing: *Describe a Picture*

ELD Standards Record Sheet

Teacher: _____ **Class:** _____

Standards: *PI.A.2*   **Guided Activities and Proficiency Levels:**

Students:	#1	#2	#3	#4	#5
_____	EM / EX / BR	EM / EX / BR	EM / EX / BR	EM / EX / BR	EM / EX / BR
_____	EM / EX / BR	EM / EX / BR	EM / EX / BR	EM / EX / BR	EM / EX / BR
_____	EM / EX / BR	EM / EX / BR	EM / EX / BR	EM / EX / BR	EM / EX / BR
_____	EM / EX / BR	EM / EX / BR	EM / EX / BR	EM / EX / BR	EM / EX / BR
_____	EM / EX / BR	EM / EX / BR	EM / EX / BR	EM / EX / BR	EM / EX / BR
_____	EM / EX / BR	EM / EX / BR	EM / EX / BR	EM / EX / BR	EM / EX / BR
_____	EM / EX / BR	EM / EX / BR	EM / EX / BR	EM / EX / BR	EM / EX / BR
_____	EM / EX / BR	EM / EX / BR	EM / EX / BR	EM / EX / BR	EM / EX / BR
_____	EM / EX / BR	EM / EX / BR	EM / EX / BR	EM / EX / BR	EM / EX / BR
_____	EM / EX / BR	EM / EX / BR	EM / EX / BR	EM / EX / BR	EM / EX / BR
_____	EM / EX / BR	EM / EX / BR	EM / EX / BR	EM / EX / BR	EM / EX / BR
_____	EM / EX / BR	EM / EX / BR	EM / EX / BR	EM / EX / BR	EM / EX / BR
_____	EM / EX / BR	EM / EX / BR	EM / EX / BR	EM / EX / BR	EM / EX / BR
_____	EM / EX / BR	EM / EX / BR	EM / EX / BR	EM / EX / BR	EM / EX / BR
_____	EM / EX / BR	EM / EX / BR	EM / EX / BR	EM / EX / BR	EM / EX / BR
_____	EM / EX / BR	EM / EX / BR	EM / EX / BR	EM / EX / BR	EM / EX / BR
_____	EM / EX / BR	EM / EX / BR	EM / EX / BR	EM / EX / BR	EM / EX / BR
_____	EM / EX / BR	EM / EX / BR	EM / EX / BR	EM / EX / BR	EM / EX / BR
_____	EM / EX / BR	EM / EX / BR	EM / EX / BR	EM / EX / BR	EM / EX / BR
_____	EM / EX / BR	EM / EX / BR	EM / EX / BR	EM / EX / BR	EM / EX / BR

Writing: *Describe a Picture*

ELD Standards Record Sheet

Teacher: _____ **Class:** _____

Standards: *PII.B.3*

Guided Activities and Proficiency Levels:

Students:	#1	#2	#3	#4	#5
	EM / EX / BR	EM / EX / BR	EM / EX / BR	EM / EX / BR	EM / EX / BR
	EM / EX / BR	EM / EX / BR	EM / EX / BR	EM / EX / BR	EM / EX / BR
	EM / EX / BR	EM / EX / BR	EM / EX / BR	EM / EX / BR	EM / EX / BR
	EM / EX / BR	EM / EX / BR	EM / EX / BR	EM / EX / BR	EM / EX / BR
	EM / EX / BR	EM / EX / BR	EM / EX / BR	EM / EX / BR	EM / EX / BR
	EM / EX / BR	EM / EX / BR	EM / EX / BR	EM / EX / BR	EM / EX / BR
	EM / EX / BR	EM / EX / BR	EM / EX / BR	EM / EX / BR	EM / EX / BR
	EM / EX / BR	EM / EX / BR	EM / EX / BR	EM / EX / BR	EM / EX / BR
	EM / EX / BR	EM / EX / BR	EM / EX / BR	EM / EX / BR	EM / EX / BR
	EM / EX / BR	EM / EX / BR	EM / EX / BR	EM / EX / BR	EM / EX / BR
	EM / EX / BR	EM / EX / BR	EM / EX / BR	EM / EX / BR	EM / EX / BR
	EM / EX / BR	EM / EX / BR	EM / EX / BR	EM / EX / BR	EM / EX / BR
	EM / EX / BR	EM / EX / BR	EM / EX / BR	EM / SEX / BR	EM / EX / BR
	EM / EX / BR	EM / EX / BR	EM / EX / BR	EM / EX / BR	EM / EX / BR
	EM / EX / BR	EM / EX / BR	EM / EX / BR	EM / EX / BR	EM / EX / BR
	EM / EX / BR	EM / EX / BR	EM / EX / BR	EM / EX / BR	EM / EX / BR
	EM / EX / BR	EM / EX / BR	EM / EX / BR	EM / EX / BR	EM / EX / BR
	EM / EX / BR	EM / EX / BR	EM / EX / BR	EM / EX / BR	EM / EX / BR
	EM / EX / BR	EM / EX / BR	EM / EX / BR	EM / EX / BR	EM / EX / BR
	EM / EX / BR	EM / EX / BR	EM / EX / BR	EM / EX / BR	EM / EX / BR

Writing: *Describe a Picture*

ELD Standards Record Sheet

Teacher: _____ **Class:** _____

Standards: *PII.B.4*   **Guided Activities and Proficiency Levels:**

Students:	#1	#2	#3	#4	#5
_____	EM / EX / BR	EM / EX / BR	EM / EX / BR	EM / EX / BR	EM / EX / BR
_____	EM / EX / BR	EM / EX / BR	EM / EX / BR	EM / EX / BR	EM / EX / BR
_____	EM / EX / BR	EM / EX / BR	EM / EX / BR	EM / EX / BR	EM / EX / BR
_____	EM / EX / BR	EM / EX / BR	EM / EX / BR	EM / EX / BR	EM / EX / BR
_____	EM / EX / BR	EM / EX / BR	EM / EX / BR	EM / EX / BR	EM / EX / BR
_____	EM / EX / BR	EM / EX / BR	EM / EX / BR	EM / EX / BR	EM / EX / BR
_____	EM / EX / BR	EM / EX / BR	EM / EX / BR	EM / EX / BR	EM / EX / BR
_____	EM / EX / BR	EM / EX / BR	EM / EX / BR	EM / EX / BR	EM / EX / BR
_____	EM / EX / BR	EM / EX / BR	EM / EX / BR	EM / EX / BR	EM / EX / BR
_____	EM / EX / BR	EM / EX / BR	EM / EX / BR	EM / EX / BR	EM / EX / BR
_____	EM / EX / BR	EM / EX / BR	EM / EX / BR	EM / EX / BR	EM / EX / BR
_____	EM / EX / BR	EM / EX / BR	EM / EX / BR	EM / EX / BR	EM / EX / BR
_____	EM / EX / BR	EM / EX / BR	EM / EX / BR	EM / EX / BR	EM / EX / BR
_____	EM / EX / BR	EM / EX / BR	EM / EX / BR	EM / EX / BR	EM / EX / BR
_____	EM / EX / BR	EM / EX / BR	EM / EX / BR	EM / EX / BR	EM / EX / BR
_____	EM / EX / BR	EM / EX / BR	EM / EX / BR	EM / EX / BR	EM / EX / BR
_____	EM / EX / BR	EM / EX / BR	EM / EX / BR	EM / EX / BR	EM / EX / BR
_____	EM / EX / BR	EM / EX / BR	EM / EX / BR	EM / EX / BR	EM / EX / BR
_____	EM / EX / BR	EM / EX / BR	EM / EX / BR	EM / EX / BR	EM / EX / BR
_____	EM / EX / BR	EM / EX / BR	EM / EX / BR	EM / EX / BR	EM / EX / BR

Writing: *Describe a Picture*

ELD Standards Record Sheet

Teacher: _____ **Class:** _____

Standards: *PII.B.5*   **Guided Activities and Proficiency Levels:**

Students:	#1	#2	#3	#4	#5
_____	EM / EX / BR	EM / EX / BR	EM / EX / BR	EM / EX / BR	EM / EX / BR
_____	EM / EX / BR	EM / EX / BR	EM / EX / BR	EM / EX / BR	EM / EX / BR
_____	EM / EX / BR	EM / EX / BR	EM / EX / BR	EM / EX / BR	EM / EX / BR
_____	EM / EX / BR	EM / EX / BR	EM / EX / BR	EM / EX / BR	EM / EX / BR
_____	EM / EX / BR	EM / EX / BR	EM / EX / BR	EM / EX / BR	EM / EX / BR
_____	EM / EX / BR	EM / EX / BR	EM / EX / BR	EM / EX / BR	EM / EX / BR
_____	EM / EX / BR	EM / EX / BR	EM / EX / BR	EM / EX / BR	EM / EX / BR
_____	EM / EX / BR	EM / EX / BR	EM / EX / BR	EM / EX / BR	EM / EX / BR
_____	EM / EX / BR	EM / EX / BR	EM / EX / BR	EM / EX / BR	EM / EX / BR
_____	EM / EX / BR	EM / EX / BR	EM / EX / BR	EM / EX / BR	EM / EX / BR
_____	EM / EX / BR	EM / EX / BR	EM / EX / BR	EM / EX / BR	EM / EX / BR
_____	EM / EX / BR	EM / EX / BR	EM / EX / BR	EM / EX / BR	EM / EX / BR
_____	EM / EX / BR	EM / EX / BCR	EM / EX / BR	EM / EX / BR	EM / EX / BR
_____	EM / EX / BR	EM / EX / BR	EM / EX / BR	EM / EX / BR	EM / EX / BR
_____	EM / EX / BR	EM / EX / BR	EM / EX / BR	EM / EX / BR	EM / EX / BR
_____	EM / EX / BR	EM / EX / BR	EM / EX / BR	EM / EX / BR	EM / EX / BR
_____	EM / EX / BR	EM / EX / BR	EM / EX / BR	EM / EX / BR	EM / EX / BR
_____	EM / EX / BR	EM / EX / BR	EM / EX / BR	EM / EX / BR	EM / EX / BR
_____	EM / EX / BR	EM / EX / BR	EM / EX / BR	EM / EX / BR	EM / EX / BR

ELD Standards Record Sheet

Teacher: _____ **Class:** _____

Standards: *PII.C.6*

Guided Activities and Proficiency Levels:

Students:	#1	#2	#3	#4	#5
	EM / EX / BR	EM / EX / BR	EM / EX / BR	EM / EX / BR	EM / EX / BR
	EM / EX / BR	EM / EX / BR	EM / EX / BR	EM / EX / BR	EM / EX / BR
	EM / EX / BR	EM / EX / BR	EM / EX / BR	EM / EX / BR	EM / EX / BR
	EM / EX / BR	EM / EX / BR	EM / EX / BR	EM / EX / BR	EM / EX / BR
	EM / EX / BR	EM / EX / BR	EM / EX / BR	EM / EX / BR	EM / EX / BR
	EM / EX / BR	EM / EX / BR	EM / EX / BR	EM / EX / BR	EM / EX / BR
	EM / EX / BR	EM / EX / BR	EM / EX / BR	EM / EX / BR	EM / EX / BR
	EM / EX / BR	EM / EX / BR	EM / EX / BR	EM / EX / BR	EM / EX / BR
	EM / EX / BR	EM / EX / BR	EM / EX / BR	EM / EX / BR	EM / EX / BR
	EM / EX / BR	EM / EX / BR	EM / EX / BR	EM / EX / BR	EM / EX / BR
	EM / EX / BR	EM / EX / BR	EM / EX / BR	EM / EX / BR	EM / EX / BR
	EM / EX / BR	EM / EX / BR	EM / EX / BR	EM / EX / BR	EM / EX / BR
	EM / EX / BR	EM / EX / BR	EM / EX / BR	EM / EX / BR	EM / EX / BR
	EM / EX / BR	EM / EX / BR	EM / EX / BR	EM / EX / BR	EM / EX / BR
	EM / EX / BR	EM / EX / BR	EM / EX / BR	EM / EX / BR	EM / EX / BR
	EM / EX / BR	EM / EX / BR	EM / EX / BR	EM / EX / BR	EM / EX / BR
	EM / EX / BR	EM / EX / BR	EM / EX / BR	EM / EX / BR	EM / EX / BR
	EM / EX / BR	EM / EX / BR	EM / EX / BR	EM / EX / BR	EM / EX / BR
	EM / EX / BR	EM / EX / BR	EM / EX / BR	EM / EX / BR	EM / EX / BR
	EM / EX / BR	EM / EX / BR	EM / EX / BR	EM / EX / BR	EM / EX / BR

ELD Standards Record Sheet

Teacher: _____   **Class:** _____

Standards: *PII.C.7*

Guided Activities and Proficiency Levels:

Students:	#1	#2	#3	#4	#5
_____	EM / EX / BR	EM / EX / BR	EM / EX / BR	EM / EX / BR	EM / EX / BR
_____	EM / EX / BR	EM / EX / BR	EM / EX / BR	EM / EX / BR	EM / EX / BR
_____	EM / EX / BR	EM / EX / BR	EM / EX / BR	EM / EX / BR	EM / EX / BR
_____	EM / EX / BR	EM / EX / BR	EM / EX / BR	EM / EX / BR	EM / EX / BR
_____	EM / EX / BR	EM / EX / BR	EM / EX / BR	EM / EX / BR	EM / EX / BR
_____	EM / EX / BR	EM / EX / BR	EM / EX / BR	EM / EX / BR	EM / EX / BR
_____	EM / EX / BR	EM / EX / BR	EM / EX / BR	EM / EX / BR	EM / EX / BR
_____	EM / EX / BR	EM / EX / BR	EM / EX / BR	EM / EX / BR	EM / EX / BR
_____	EM / EX / BR	EM / EX / BR	EM / EX / BR	EM / EX / BR	EM / EX / BR
_____	EM / EX / BR	EM / EX / BR	EM / EX / BR	EM / EX / BR	EM / EX / BR
_____	EM / EX / BR	EM / EX / BR	EM / EX / BR	EM / EX / BR	EM / EX / BR
_____	EM / EX / BR	EM / EX / BR	EM / EX / BR	EM / EX / BR	EM / EX / BR
_____	EM / EX / BR	EM / EX / BR	EM / EX / BR	EM / EX / BR	EM / EX / BR
_____	EM / EX / BR	EM / EX / BR	EM / EX / BR	EM / EX / BR	EM / EX / BR
_____	EM / EX / BR	EM / EX / BR	EM / EX / BR	EM / EX / BR	EM / EX / BR
_____	EM / EX / BR	EM / EX / BR	EM / EX / BR	EM / EX / BR	EM / EX / BR
_____	EM / EX / BR	EM / EX / BR	EM / EX / BR	EM / EX / BR	EM / EX / BR
_____	EM / EX / BR	EM / EX / BR	EM / EX / BR	EM / EX / BR	EM / EX / BR
_____	EM / EX / BR	EM / EX / BR	EM / EX / BR	EM / EX / BR	EM / EX / BR

Writing Practice #1

Name: _____

Directions: Look at the picture. Then read the paragraph that has been written about the picture. Follow the directions to correct any errors and add details. You can use any vocabulary words from the list provided.

Vocabulary

wagon
playing
park
city
dog
chasing
exciting

The kids are taking turns. The girl holded on as she rided. The boy was holding the handle. He was pulling.

---

1 Look at this sentence.

The kids are taking turns.

Rewrite this sentence with more details.

_____

_____

_____

_____

_____

Writing Activity #1 - cont'd

2 Look at this sentence.

The girl holded on as she rided.

The sentence has TWO errors. Rewrite the sentence correctly.

_____

_____

_____

_____

_____

3 Look at these two sentences.

The boy was holding the handle. He was pulling.

Combine the two sentences into one.

_____

_____

_____

_____

_____

4 Write another sentence to describe the picture with more details.

_____

_____

_____

_____

_____

Writing Practice #2

Name: _____

Directions: Look at the picture. Then read the paragraph that has been written about the picture. Follow the directions to correct any errors and add details. You can use any vocabulary words from the list provided.

Vocabulary

playground
jump rope
sunny
outside
jungle gym
school
friends

> **The students are at recess. The boy is have fun jumped up high. The girl is next to jump rope. She is excited.**

1	Look at this sentence.

The students are at recess.

Rewrite this sentence with more details.

_____

_____

_____

_____

_____

Writing Activity #2 - cont'd

2 Look at this sentence.

The boy is have fun jumped up high.

The sentence has TWO errors. Rewrite the sentence correctly.

_____

_____

_____

_____

_____

3 Look at these two sentences.

The girl is next to jump rope. She is excited.

Combine the two sentences into one.

_____

_____

_____

_____

_____

4 Write another sentence to describe the picture with more details.

_____

_____

_____

_____

_____

Writing: *Describe a Picture*

Writing Practice #3

Name: _____

Directions: Look at the picture. Then read the paragraph that has been written about the picture. Follow the directions to correct any errors and add details. You can use any vocabulary words from the list provided.

Vocabulary

lemonade
pitcher
stand
sign
straws
bought
fundraising

The kids are selling. The girl just bringed a hole bag of lemons. The boy is giving the man a glass. It is a glass of lemonade.

---

1 Look at this sentence.

The kids are selling.

Rewrite this sentence with more details.

_____

_____

_____

_____

_____

30

Writing Activity #3 - cont'd

2 Look at this sentence.

The girl just bringed a hole bag of lemons.

The sentence has TWO errors. Rewrite the sentence correctly.

_____

_____

_____

_____

_____

3 Look at these two sentences.

The boy is giving the man a glass. It is a glass of lemonade.

Combine the two sentences into one.

_____

_____

_____

_____

_____

4 Write another sentence to describe the picture with more details.

_____

_____

_____

_____

Writing Practice #4

Name: _____

Directions: Look at the picture. Then read the paragraph that has been written about the picture. Follow the directions to correct any errors and add details. You can use any vocabulary words from the list provided.

Vocabulary

crosswalk
traffic light
safe
stop sign
bags
caution
safety vest

The students are going to school. The crossing guard is careful held the sign. The cars are stopped. The students can cross.

---

1 Look at this sentence.

The students are going to school.

Rewrite this sentence with more details.

_____

_____

_____

_____

_____

Writing Activity #4 - cont'd

2   Look at this sentence.

The crossing guard is careful held the sign.

The sentence has TWO errors. Rewrite the sentence correctly.

_____

_____

_____

_____

_____

_____

3   Look at these two sentences.

The cars are stopped. The students can cross.

Combine the two sentences into one.

_____

_____

_____

_____

_____

4   Write another sentence to describe the picture with more details.

_____

_____

_____

_____

_____

Writing Practice #5

Name: _____

Directions: Look at the picture. Then read the paragraph that has been written about the picture. Follow the directions to correct any errors and add details. You can use any vocabulary words from the list provided.

Vocabulary

park
breezy
blowing
fun
leash
clouds
trees

It is a windy day. The kids runned fast to fly there kites. The lady is walking. She is with a dog.

---

1 Look at this sentence.

It is a windy day.

Rewrite this sentence with more details.

_____

_____

_____

_____

_____

Writing Activity #5 - cont'd

2 Look at this sentence.

The kids runned fast to fly there kites.

The sentence has TWO errors. Rewrite the sentence correctly.

_____

_____

_____

_____

_____

3 Look at these two sentences.

The lady is walking. She is with a dog.

Combine the two sentences into one.

_____

_____

_____

_____

_____

4 Write another sentence to describe the picture with more details.

_____

_____

_____

_____

Writing
Write About an Experience

This section includes:
- Guided Activities
- Teacher's ELD Standards Record Sheet
- Student Practice Activities:
  - Graphic organizers
  - Personal experience writing practice
  - Bonus blank writing template

Alignment to CA ELD Standards:

Alignment to CCSS:

Part I: Interacting in Meaningful Ways

C.10 Writing
Writing literary and informational texts to present, describe, and explain ideas and information, using appropriate technology

W.3.1–8, 10; L.3.1–3, 6
W.4.1–10; L.4.1–3, 6
W.5.1–10; L.5.1–3, 6

Part II: Learning About How English Works

B.3 Expanding and Enriching Ideas
Using verbs and verb phrases

W.3.5; SL.3.6; L.3.1, 3, 6
W.4.5; SL.4.6; L.4.1, 3, 6
W.5.5; SL.5.6; L.5.1, 3, 6

Part II: Learning About How English Works

B.4 Expanding and Enriching Ideas
Using nouns and noun phrases

W.3.5; SL.3.6; L.3.1, 3, 6
W.4.5; SL.4.6; L.4.1, 3, 6
W.5.5; SL.5.6; L.5.1, 3, 6

Part II: Learning About How English Works

B.5 Expanding and Enriching Ideas
Modifying to add details

W.3.5; SL.3.4, 6; L.3.1, 3, 6
W.4.5; SL.4.4, 6; L.4.1, 3, 6
W.5.5; SL.5.4, 6; L.5.1, 3, 6

Part II: Learning About How English Works

C.6 Connecting and Condensing Ideas
Connecting ideas

W.3.1-3, 5; SL.3.4, 6; L.3.1, 3, 6
W.4.1–3, 5; SL.4.4, 6; L.4.1, 3, 6
W.5.1–3, 5; SL.5.4, 6; L.5.1, 3, 6

Writing
Write About an Experience

Guided Activities Direction:

1. Show students the writing prompt
2. Explain to the students that they'll be writing about a familiar topic based on their personal experience
3. Guide students through:
   - Reading the directions and prompt carefully
   - Understanding what should be included in their writing
   - Understanding if revisions to their writing is necessary
4. Then have students practice with additional writing activities for personal experiences.

....

Guiding Descriptors
Use the following guidelines to assist students with their writing.

- Guide students in providing a description of the experience mentioned in the prompt

- Guide students in using well-developed descriptions, details, and/or examples

- Help students make sure that their response is readily coherent

- Help students with their grammar and word choice

- Help students with their spelling and punctuation

- Guide students in writing a response that includes a paragraph of at least three sentences

Writing: *Write About an Experience*

Guided Activity #1

Name: _____

Directions: You are going to write a paragraph in English about your personal experience.

- Your paragraph should include at least THREE complete sentences
- Include a beginning, middle, and end
- Be sure to use descriptions, details, and examples to make your writing interesting
- Check your writing for correct grammar, capital letters, punctuation, and spelling
- Do not write outside the box
- Make sure your writing is neat and legible

Writing Prompt: *Think about a time when you tried something new. What was it? Why did you decide to try it? How did you feel? What was the experience like for you?*

Guided Activity #2

Name: _____

Directions: You are going to write a paragraph in English about your personal experience.
- Your paragraph should include at least THREE complete sentences
- Include a beginning, middle, and end
- Be sure to use descriptions, details, and examples to make your writing interesting
- Check your writing for correct grammar, capital letters, punctuation, and spelling
- Do not write outside the box
- Make sure your writing is neat and legible

Writing Prompt: *Think about a time when you helped a friend. Why did your friend need help? How did you help your friend? How did you feel?*

Guided Activity #3

Name: _____

Directions: You are going to write a paragraph in English about your personal experience.

- Your paragraph should include at least THREE complete sentences
- Include a beginning, middle, and end
- Be sure to use descriptions, details, and examples to make your writing interesting
- Check your writing for correct grammar, capital letters, punctuation, and spelling
- Do not write outside the box
- Make sure your writing is neat and legible

Writing Prompt: *Think about a time when you had a lot of fun with your family. What did you and your family do? What made it fun? How did it make you feel?*

Guided Activity #4

Name: _____

Directions: You are going to write a paragraph in English about your personal experience.

- Your paragraph should include at least THREE complete sentences
- Include a beginning, middle, and end
- Be sure to use descriptions, details, and examples to make your writing interesting
- Check your writing for correct grammar, capital letters, punctuation, and spelling
- Do not write outside the box
- Make sure your writing is neat and legible

Writing Prompt: *Think about a time when you felt scared or nervous. What made you feel this way? Why did you feel this way? How did you overcome this feeling?*

Guided Activity #5

Name: ....

Directions: You are going to write a paragraph in English about your personal experience.

- Your paragraph should include at least THREE complete sentences
- Include a beginning, middle, and end
- Be sure to use descriptions, details, and examples to make your writing interesting
- Check your writing for correct grammar, capital letters, punctuation, and spelling
- Do not write outside the box
- Make sure your writing is neat and legible

Writing Prompt: *Think about a time when you watched a really good movie. What was the movie about? Why did you enjoy the movie? How did it make you feel?*

ELD Standards Record Sheet

<u>Directions:</u>

1. Look at the CA ELD standards (**BELOW**) that correspond to this section.
2. Reference these specific standards for the template Record Sheet.
3. Use the following template Record Sheet to monitor students' proficiency levels for the **GUIDED ACTIVITIES** in this section.
4. Fill out all the information. Circle, check, highlight the proficiency level. (*There is space for 20 students. Make additional copies, as needed*)
5. Retain for your records to be used during grading, parent/student conferences, lesson planning, ELD documentation, etc.

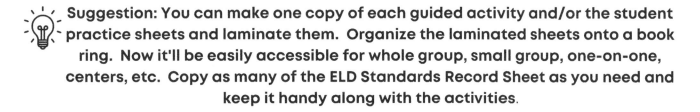 **Suggestion: You can make one copy of each guided activity and/or the student practice sheets and laminate them. Organize the laminated sheets onto a book ring. Now it'll be easily accessible for whole group, small group, one-on-one, centers, etc. Copy as many of the ELD Standards Record Sheet as you need and keep it handy along with the activities**.

Writing: *Write About an Experience*

ELD Standards Record Sheet
CA ELD Standards & Proficiency Levels
Part I: Interacting in Meaningful Ways
C.10 Writing

EMERGING (EM)	EXPANDING (EX)	BRIDGING (BR)
*Requires **Substantial** Support*	*Requires **Moderate** Support*	*Requires **Light** Support*

GRADE 3

EMERGING (EM)	EXPANDING (EX)	BRIDGING (BR)
• Write short literary texts • Write short informational texts (e.g. a description of a flashlight) • Use familiar vocabulary • Collaborate with an adult, peers, and sometimes independently (e.g. joint construction of texts) • Paraphrase texts and recount experiences using key words from notes or graphic organizers	• Write <u>longer</u> literary texts • Write <u>longer</u> informational texts (e.g. an explanatory text on how flashlights works) • Use <u>expanded</u> vocabulary <u>to provide information</u> • Collaborate with an adult, peers, and with <u>increasing</u> independence <u>using appropriate text organization</u> (e.g. joint construction of texts) • Paraphrase texts and recount experiences using <u>complete sentences</u> and key words from notes or graphic organizers	• Write longer and <u>more detailed</u> literary texts • Write longer and <u>more detailed</u> informational texts (e.g. an explanatory text on how flashlights work) • <u>Write and express ideas to meet specific purposes and audiences</u> • Collaborate with an adult, peers, and <u>independently</u> using appropriate text organization and <u>growing understanding of register.</u> • Paraphrase texts and recount experiences using <u>increasingly detailed complete sentences</u> and key words from notes or graphic organizers

GRADE 4

EMERGING (EM)	EXPANDING (EX)	BRIDGING (BR)

• Write short literary texts
• Write short informational texts (e.g. a description of a flashlight)
• Use familiar vocabulary
• Collaborate with an adult, peers, and sometimes independently (e.g. joint construction of texts)
• Write brief summaries of texts and experiences using:
   ◦ Complete sentences
   ◦ Key words (e.g. from notes or graphic organizers)
	• Write <u>longer</u> literary texts
	• Write <u>longer</u> informational texts (e.g. an explanatory text on how flashlights works)
	• Use <u>expanded</u> vocabulary <u>to provide information</u>
	• Collaborate with an adult, peers, and with <u>increasing independence</u> <u>using appropriate text organization</u> (e.g. joint construction of texts)
	• Write <u>increasingly concise</u> summaries of texts and experiences using:
	   ◦ Complete sentences
	   ◦ Key words (e.g. from notes or graphic organizers)
		• Write longer and <u>more detailed</u> literary texts
		• Write longer and <u>more detailed</u> informational texts (e.g. an explanatory text on how flashlights work)
		• <u>Write and express ideas to meet specific purposes and audiences</u>
		• Collaborate with an adult, peers, and <u>independently</u> using appropriate text organization and <u>growing understanding of register.</u>(e.g. joint construction of texts)
		• Write <u>clear and coherent</u> summaries of texts and experiences using:
		   ◦ Complete and <u>concise</u> sentences
		   ◦ Key words (e.g. from notes or graphic organizers)

GRADE 5

EMERGING (EM)	EXPANDING (EX)	BRIDGING (BR)

• Write short literary texts
• Write short informational texts (e.g. a description of a camel)
• Use familiar vocabulary
• Collaborate with an adult, peers, and sometimes independently (e.g. joint construction of texts)
• Write brief summaries of texts and experiences using:
   ◦ Complete sentences
   ◦ Key words (e.g. from notes or graphic organizers)
	• Write <u>longer</u> literary texts
	• Write <u>longer</u> informational texts (e.g. an informative report on different kinds of camels)
	• Use <u>expanded</u> vocabulary <u>to provide information</u>
	• Collaborate with an adult, peers, and with <u>increasing</u> independence <u>using appropriate text organization</u> (e.g. joint construction of texts)
	• Write <u>increasingly concise</u> summaries of texts and experiences using:
	   ◦ Complete sentences
	   ◦ Key words (e.g. from notes or graphic organizers)
		• Write longer and <u>more detailed</u> literary texts
		• Write longer and <u>more detailed</u> informational texts (e.g. an explanation of how camels survive without water for a long time)
		• <u>Write and express ideas to meet specific purposes and audiences</u>
		• Collaborate with an adult, peers, and <u>independently</u> using appropriate text organization and <u>growing understanding of register.</u> (e.g. joint construction of texts)
		• Write <u>clear and coherent</u> summaries of texts and experiences using:
		   ◦ Complete and <u>concise</u> sentences
		   ◦ Key words (e.g. from notes or graphic organizers)

Writing: *Write About an Experience*

ELD Standards Record Sheet

CA ELD Standards & Proficiency Levels

Part II: Learning About How English Works
B.3 Using Verbs and Verb Phrases

EMERGING (EM)→	► EXPANDING (EX) →	► BRIDGING (BR)
*Requires **Substantial** Support*	*Requires **Moderate** Support*	*Requires **Light** Support*
	GRADE 3	
• *Use frequently used verbs* • *Use different verb types (e.g. doing, saying, being/having, thinking/feeling)* • *Use different verb tenses (e.g. simple past for recounting an experience)* • *Appropriate for the text type and discipline to convey time*	• *Use a <u>growing number</u> of verb types (e.g. doing, saying, being/having, thinking/feeling)* • *Use a <u>growing number</u> of verb tenses (e.g. simple past for retelling, simple present for a science description)* • *Appropriate for the text type and discipline to convey time*	• *Use a <u>variety</u> of verb types (e.g. doing, saying, being/having, thinking/feeling)* • *Use a <u>variety</u> of verb tenses (e.g. simple present for a science description, simple future to predict)* • *Appropriate for the text type and discipline to convey time*
	GRADE 4	
• *Use various verbs* • *Use various verb types (e.g. doing, saying, being/having, thinking/feeling)* • *Use various verb tenses (e.g. simple past for recounting an experience)* • *Appropriate for the text type and discipline for familiar topics*	• *Use various verbs* • *Use various verb types (e.g. doing, saying, being/having, thinking/feeling)* • *Use various verb tenses (e.g. simple past for retelling, timeless present for science explanation)* • *Appropriate for the <u>task</u>, text type and discipline* • *<u>For an increasing variety of familiar and new topics</u>*	• *Use various verb* • *Use various verb types (e.g. doing, saying, being/having, thinking/feeling)* • *Use various verb tenses(e.g. timeless present for science explanation, mixture of past and present for historical information report)* • *Appropriate for the task and text type* • *For a <u>variety</u> of familiar and new topics*
	GRADE 5	
• *Use frequently used verbs (e.g. take, like, eat)* • *Use various verb types (e.g. doing, saying, being/having, thinking/feeling)* • *Use various verb tenses (e.g. simple past for recounting an experience)* • *Appropriate for the text type and discipline for familiar topics*	• *Use <u>various</u> verb types (e.g. doing, saying, being/having, thinking/feeling)* • *Use various verb tenses (e.g. simple past for retelling, timeless present for science a description)* • *Appropriate for the <u>task</u>, text type and discipline* • *<u>For an increasing variety of topics</u>*	• *Use various verb types (e.g. doing, saying, being/having, thinking/feeling)* • *Use various verb tenses (e.g. timeless present for science description, mixture of past and present for narrative or history explanation)* • *Appropriate for the task and text type* • *For a <u>variety</u> of topics*

ELD Standards Record Sheet

CA ELD Standards & Proficiency Levels

Part II: Learning About How English Works
B.4 Using Nouns and Noun Phrases

EMERGING (EM)	EXPANDING (EX)	BRIDGING (BR)
Requires **Substantial** Support	Requires **Moderate** Support	Requires **Light** Support
GRADE 3		
• Expand noun phrases in simple ways in order to enrich: ◦ The meaning of sentences ◦ Add details about ideas, people, things, etc. (e.g. adding an adjective to a noun)	• Expand noun phrases in a _growing number_ of ways in order to enrich: ◦ The meaning of sentences ◦ Add details about ideas, people, things, etc. (e.g. adding comparative/superlative adjectives to nouns)	• Expand noun phrases in a _variety_ of ways in order to enrich: ◦ The meaning of sentences and ◦ Add details about ideas, people, things, etc. (e.g. adding comparative/superlative adjectives to nouns, simple clause embedding)
GRADE 4		
• Expand noun phrases in simple ways in order to enrich: ◦ The meaning of sentences ◦ Add details about ideas, people, things, etc. (e.g. adding an adjective)	• Expand noun phrases in a _variety_ of ways in order to enrich: ◦ The meaning of sentences ◦ Add details about ideas, people, things, etc. (e.g. adding adjectives to noun phrases or simple clause embedding)	• Expand noun phrases in an _increasing variety_ of ways in order to enrich: ◦ The meaning of sentences and ◦ Add details about ideas, people, things, etc. (e.g. adding general academic adjectives and adverbs to noun phrases or more complex clause embedding)
GRADE 5		
• Expand noun phrases in simple ways in order to enrich: ◦ The meaning of sentences ◦ Add details about ideas, people, things, etc. (e.g. adding an adjective to a noun)	• Expand noun phrases in a _variety_ of ways in order to enrich: ◦ The meaning of sentences ◦ Add details about ideas, people, things, etc. (e.g. adding comparative/superlative adjectives to noun phrases or simple clause embedding)	• Expand noun phrases in an _increasing variety_ of ways in order to enrich: ◦ The meaning of sentences ◦ Add details about ideas, people, things, etc. (e.g. adding comparative/superlative and general academic adjectives to noun phrases or more complex clause embedding)

ELD Standards Record Sheet

CA ELD Standards & Proficiency Levels

Part II: Learning About How English Works
B.5 Modifying to Add Details

EMERGING (EM)	EXPANDING (EX)	BRIDGING (BR)
Requires **Substantial** Support	Requires **Moderate** Support	Requires **Light** Support
GRADE 3		
• Expand sentences with adverbials (e.g. adverbs, adverb phrases, prepositional phrases) • Use these to provide details about a familiar activity or process (e.g. time, manner, place, cause) (e.g. They walked to the soccer field.)	• Expand sentences with adverbials (e.g. adverbs, adverb phrases, prepositional phrases) • Use these to provide details about a familiar or <u>new activity</u> or process (e.g. time, manner, place, cause) (e.g. They worked quietly; They ran across the soccer field.)	• Expand sentences with adverbials (e.g. adverbs, adverb phrases, prepositional phrases) • Use these to provide details about a <u>range</u> of familiar and new activities or processes.(e.g. time, manner, place, cause) (e.g. They worked quietly all night in their room.)
GRADE 4		
• Expand sentences with familiar adverbials (e.g. basic prepositional phrases) • Use these to provide details about a familiar activity or process (e.g. time, manner, place, cause) (e.g. They walked to the soccer field.)	• Expand sentences with a <u>growing variety</u> of adverbials (e.g. adverbs, prepositional phrases) • Use these to provide details about a familiar or <u>new activity</u> or process (e.g. time, manner, place, cause) (e.g. They worked quietly; They ran across the soccer field.)	• Expand sentences with a <u>variety</u> of adverbials (e.g. adverbs, adverb phrases, prepositional phrases) • Use these to provide details about a <u>variety</u> of familiar and new activities or processes.(e.g. time, manner, place, cause) (e.g. They worked quietly all night in their room.)
GRADE 5		
• Expand and enrich sentences with adverbials (e.g. adverbs, adverb phrases, prepositional phrases) • Use these to provide details about a familiar activity or process (e.g. time, manner, place, cause)	• Expand and enrich sentences with adverbials (e.g. adverbs, adverb phrases, prepositional phrases) • Use these to provide details about a familiar or <u>new activity</u> or process (e.g. time, manner, place, cause)	• Expand and enrich sentences with adverbials (e.g. adverbs, adverb phrases, prepositional phrases) • Use these to provide details about a <u>variety</u> of familiar and new activities or processes.(e.g. time, manner, place, cause)

Writing: *Write About an Experience*

ELD Standards Record Sheet

CA ELD Standards & Proficiency Levels
Part II: Learning About How English Works
C.6 Connecting Ideas

EMERGING (EM) —	EXPANDING (EX) —	BRIDGING (BR)
*Requires **Substantial** Support*	*Requires **Moderate** Support*	*Requires **Light** Support*
	GRADE 3	

• *Combine clauses in a few basic ways*
• *To make connections between and to join ideas (e.g. creating compound sentences using and, but, so)*
	• *Combine clauses in an <u>increasing variety</u> of ways (e.g. creating compound and complex sentences)*
	• *to make connections between and to join ideas, for example:*
	  ◦ *<u>to express cause/effect (e.g. The deer ran because the mountain lion came.)</u>*
	  ◦ *<u>to make a concession (e.g. She studied all night even though she wasn't feeling well.)</u>*
		• *Combine clauses in a <u>wide variety</u> of ways (e.g. creating compound and complex sentences)*
		• *to make connections between and to join ideas, for example:*
		  ◦ *to express cause/effect (e.g. The deer ran because the mountain lion approached them.)*
		  ◦ *to make a concession(e.g. She studied all night even though she wasn't feeling well.)*
		  ◦ *<u>to link two ideas that happen at the same time (e.g. The cubs played while their mother hunted.)</u>*

	GRADE 4	

• *Combine clauses in a few basic ways*
• *To make connections between and to join ideas in sentences (e.g. creating compound sentences using coordinate conjunctions, such as and, but, so)*
	• *Combine clauses in an <u>increasing variety</u> of ways (e.g. creating complex sentences using familiar subordinate conjunctions)*
	• *to make connections between and to join ideas in sentences, for example:*
	  ◦ *<u>to express cause/effect (e.g. The deer ran because the mountain lion came.)</u>*
	  ◦ *<u>to make a concession (e.g. She studied all night even though she wasn't feeling well.)</u>*
		• *Combine clauses in a <u>wide variety</u> of ways (e.g. creating complex sentences using a variety of subordinate conjunctions)*
		• *to make connections between and to join ideas, for example:*
		  ◦ *to express cause/effect (e.g. Since the lion was at the waterhole, the deer ran away.)*
		  ◦ *to make a concession*
		  ◦ *<u>to link two ideas that happen at the same time (e.g. The cubs played while their mother hunted.)</u>*

	GRADE 5	

• *Combine clauses in a few basic ways*
• *To make connections between and to join ideas*
• *To provide evidence to support ideas or opinions (e.g. You must X because X.) (e.g. creating compound sentences using and, but, so)*
	• *Combine clauses in an <u>increasing variety</u> of ways (e.g. creating compound and complex sentences)*
	• *to make connections between and to join ideas, for example:*
	  ◦ *<u>to express cause/effect (e.g. The deer ran because the mountain lion came.)</u>*
	  ◦ *<u>to make a concession(e.g. She studied all night even though she wasn't feeling well.)</u>*
	• *To provide reasons to support ideas (e.g. X is an extremely good book because X)*
		• *Combine clauses in a <u>wide variety</u> of ways (e.g. creating compound and complex sentences)*
		• *to make connections between and to join ideas, for example:*
		  ◦ *to express cause/effect (e.g. The deer ran because the mountain lion approached them.)*
		  ◦ *to make a concession (e.g. She studied all night even though she wasn't feeling well.)*
		  ◦ *<u>to link two ideas that happen at the same time (e.g. The cubs played while their mother hunted.)</u>*
		• *To provide reasons to support ideas (e.g The author persuades the reader by X.)*

Writing: *Write About an Experience*

ELD Standards Record Sheet

Teacher: _____ **Class:** _____

Standards: *PI.C.10*   **Guided Activities and Proficiency Levels:**

Students:	#1	#2	#3	#4	#5
_____	EM / EX / BR	EM / EX / BR	EM / EX / BR	EM / EX / BR	EM / EX / BR
_____	EM / EX / BR	EM / EX / BR	EM / EX / BR	EM / EX / BR	EM / EX / BR
_____	EM / EX / BR	EM / EX / BR	EM / EX / BR	EM / EX / BR	EM / EX / BR
_____	EM / EX / BR	EM / EX / BR	EM / EX / BR	EM / EX / BR	EM / EX / BR
_____	EM / EX / BR	EM / EX / BR	EM / EX / BR	EM / EX / BR	EM / EX / BR
_____	EM / EX / BR	EM / EX / BR	EM / EX / BR	EM / EX / BR	EM / EX / BR
_____	EM / EX / BR	EM / EX / BR	EM / EX / BR	EM / EX / BR	EM / EX / BR
_____	EM / EX / BR	EM / EX / BR	EM / EX / BR	EM / EX / BR	EM / EX / BR
_____	EM / EX / BR	EM / EX / BR	EM / EX / BR	EM / EX / BR	EM / EX / BR
_____	EM / EX / BR	EM / EX / BR	EM / EX / BR	EM / EX / BR	EM / EX / BR
_____	EM / EX / BR	EM / EX / BR	EM / EX / BR	EM / EX / BR	EM / EX / BR
_____	EM / EX / BR	EM / EX / BR	EM / EX / BR	EM / EX / BR	EM / EX / BR
_____	EM / EX / BR	EM / EX / BR	EM / EX / BR	EM / EX / BR	EM / EX / BR
_____	EM / EX / BR	EM / EX / BR	EM / EX / BR	EM / EX / BR	EM / EX / BR
_____	EM / EX / BR	EM / EX / BR	EM / EX / BR	EM / EX / BR	EM / EX / BR
_____	EM / EX / BR	EM / EX / BR	EM / EX / BR	EM / EX / BR	EM / EX / BR
_____	EM / EX / BR	EM / EX / BR	EM / EX / BR	EM / EX / BR	EM / EX / BR
_____	EM / EX / BR	EM / EX / BR	EM / EX / BR	EM / EX / BR	EM / EX / BR
_____	EM / EX / BR	EM / EX / BR	EM / EX / BR	EM / EX / BR	EM / EX / BR
_____	EM / EX / BR	EM / EX / BR	EM / EX / BR	EM / EX / BR	EM / EX / BR

ELD Standards Record Sheet

Teacher: _____ **Class:** _____

Standards: *PII.B.3*

Guided Activities and Proficiency Levels:

Students:	#1	#2	#3	#4	#5
	EM / EX / BR	EM / EX / BR	EM / EX / BR	EM / EX / BR	EM / EX / BR
	EM / EX / BR	EM / EX / BR	EM / EX / BR	EM / EX / BR	EM / EX / BR
	EM / EX / BR	EM / EX / BR	EM / EX / BR	EM / EX / BR	EM / EX / BR
	EM / EX / BR	EM / EX / BR	EM / EX / BR	EM / EX / BR	EM / EX / BR
	EM / EX / BR	EM / EX / BR	EM / EX / BR	EM / EX / BR	EM / EX / BR
	EM / EX / BR	EM / EX / BR	EM / EX / BR	EM / EX / BR	EM / EX / BR
	EM / EX / BR	EM / EX / BR	EM / EX / BR	EM / EX / BR	EM / EX / BR
	EM / EX / BR	EM / EX / BR	EM / EX / BR	EM / EX / BR	EM / EX / BR
	EM / EX / BR	EM / EX / BR	EM / EX / BR	EM / EX / BR	EM / EX / BR
	EM / EX / BR	EM / EX / BR	EM / EX / BR	EM / EX / BR	EM / EX / BR
	EM / EX / BR	EM / EX / BR	EM / EX / BR	EM / EX / BR	EM / EX / BR
	EM / EX / BR	EM / EX / BR	EM / EX / BR	EM / EX / BR	EM / EX / BR
	EM / EX / BR	EM / EX / BR	EM / EX / BR	EM / EX / BR	EM / EX / BR
	EM / EX / BR	EM / EX / BR	EM / EX / BR	EM / EX / BR	EM / EX / BR
	EM / EX / BR	EM / EX / BR	EM / EX / BR	EM / EX / BR	EM / EX / BR
	EM / EX / BR	EM / EX / BR	EM / EX / BR	EM / EX / BR	EM / EX / BR
	EM / EX / BR	EM / EX / BR	EM / EX / BR	EM / EX / BR	EM / EX / BR
	EM / EX / BR	EM / EX / BR	EM / EX / BR	EM / EX / BR	EM / EX / BR
	EM / EX / BR	EM / EX / BR	EM / EX / BR	EM / EX / BR	EM / EX / BR
	EM / EX / BR	EM / EX / BR	EM / EX / BR	EM / EX / BR	EM / EX / BR

Writing: *Write About an Experience*

ELD Standards Record Sheet

Teacher: _____ **Class:** _____

Standards: *PII.B.4*

Guided Activities and Proficiency Levels:

Students:	#1	#2	#3	#4	#5
	EM / EX / BR	EM / EX / BR	EM / EX / BR	EM / EX / BR	EM / EX / BR
	EM / EX / BR	EM / EX / BR	EM / EX / BR	EM / EX / BR	EM / EX / BR
	EM / EX / BR	EM / EX / BR	EM / EX / BR	EM / EX / BR	EM / EX / BR
	EM / EX / BR	EM / EX / BR	EM / EX / BR	EM / EX / BR	EM / EX / BR
	EM / EX / BR	EM / EX / BR	EM / EX / BR	EM / EX / BR	EM / EX / BR
	EM / EX / BR	EM / EX / BR	EM / EX / BR	EM / EX / BR	EM / EX / BR
	EM / EX / BR	EM / EX / BR	EM / EX / BR	EM / EX / BR	EM / EX / BR
	EM / EX / BR	EM / EX / BR	EM / EX / BR	EM / EX / BR	EM / EX / BR
	EM / EX / BR	EM / EX / BR	EM / EX / BR	EM / EX / BR	EM / EX / BR
	EM / EX / BR	EM / EX / BR	EM / EX / BR	EM / EX / BR	EM / EX / BR
	EM / EX / BR	EM / EX / BR	EM / EX / BR	EM / EX / BR	EM / EX / BR
	EM / EX / BR	EM / EX / BR	EM / EX / BR	EM / EX / BR	EM / EX / BR
	EM / EX / BR	EM / EX / BR	EM / EX / BR	EM / EX / BR	EM / EX / BR
	EM / EX / BR	EM / EX / BR	EM / EX / BR	EM / EX / BR	EM / EX / BR
	EM / EX / BR	EM / EX / BR	EM / EX / BR	EM / EX / BR	EM / EX / BR
	EM / EX / BR	EM / EX / BR	EM / EX / BR	EM / EX / BR	EM / EX / BR
	EM / EX / BR	EM / EX / BR	EM / EX / BR	EM / EX / BR	EM / EX / BR
	EM / EX / BR	EM / EX / BR	EM / EX / BR	EM / EX / BR	EM / EX / BR
	EM / EX / BR	EM / EX / BR	EM / EX / BR	EM / EX / BR	EM / EX / BR
	EM / EX / BR	EM / EX / BR	EM / EX / BR	EM / EX / BR	EM / EX / BR

ELD Standards Record Sheet

Teacher: _____ **Class:** _____

Standards: *PII.B.5*

Guided Activities and Proficiency Levels:

Students:	#1	#2	#3	#4	#5
_____	EM / EX / BR	EM / EX / BR	EM / EX / BR	EM / EX / BR	EM / EX / BR
_____	EM / EX / BR	EM / EX / BR	EM / EX / BR	EM / EX / BR	EM / EX / BR
_____	EM / EX / BR	EM / EX / BR	EM / EX / BR	EM / EX / BR	EM / EX / BR
_____	EM / EX / BR	EM / EX / BR	EM / EX / BR	EM / EX / BR	EM / EX / BR
_____	EM / EX / BR	EM / EX / BR	EM / EX / BR	EM / EX / BR	EM / EX / BR
_____	EM / EX / BR	EM / EX / BR	EM / EX / BR	EM / EX / BR	EM / EX / BR
_____	EM / EX / BR	EM / EX / BR	EM / EX / BR	EM / EX / BR	EM / EX / BR
_____	EM / EX / BR	EM / EX / BR	EM / EX / BR	EM / EX / BR	EM / EX / BR
_____	EM / EX / BR	EM / EX / BR	EM / EX / BR	EM / EX / BR	EM / EX / BR
_____	EM / EX / BR	EM / EX / BR	EM / EX / BR	EM / EX / BR	EM / EX / BR
_____	EM / EX / BR	EM / EX / BR	EM / EX / BR	EM / EX / BR	EM / EX / BR
_____	EM / EX / BR	EM / EX / BR	EM / EX / BR	EM / EX / BR	EM / EX / BR
_____	EM / EX / BR	EM / EX / BR	EM / EX / BR	EM / EX / BR	EM / EX / BR
_____	EM / EX / BR	EM / EX / BR	EM / EX / BR	EM / EX / BR	EM / EX / BR
_____	EM / EX / BR	EM / EX / BR	EM / EX / BR	EM / EX / BR	EM / EX / BR
_____	EM / EX / BR	EM / EX / BR	EM / EX / BR	EM / EX / BR	EM / EX / BR
_____	EM / EX / BR	EM / EX / BR	EM / EX / BR	EM / EX / BR	EM / EX / BR
_____	EM / EX / BR	EM / EX / BR	EM / EX / BR	EM / EX / BR	EM / EX / BR
_____	EM / EX / BR	EM / EX / BR	EM / EX / BR	EM / EX / BR	EM / EX / BR
_____	EM / EX / BR	EM / EX / BR	EM / EX / BR	EM / EX / BR	EM / EX / BR

Writing: *Write About an Experience*

ELD Standards Record Sheet

Teacher: _____ **Class:** _____

Standards: *PII.C.6* **Guided Activities and Proficiency Levels:**

Students:	#1	#2	#3	#4	#5
_____	EM / EX / BR	EM / EX / BR	EM / EX / BR	EM / EX / BR	EM / EX / BR
_____	EM / EX / BR	EM / EX / BR	EM / EX / BR	EM / EX / BR	EM / EX / BR
_____	EM / EX / BR	EM / EX / BR	EM / EX / BR	EM / EX / BR	EM / EX / BR
_____	EM / EX / BR	EM / EX / BR	EM / EX / BR	EM / EX / BR	EM / EX / BR
_____	EM / EX / BR	EM / EX / BR	EM / EX / BR	EM / EX / BR	EM / EX / BR
_____	EM / EX / BR	EM / EX / BR	EM / EX / BR	EM / EX / BR	EM / EX / BR
_____	EM / EX / BR	EM / EX / BR	EM / EX / BR	EM / EX / BR	EM / EX / BR
_____	EM / EX / BR	EM / EX / BR	EM / EX / BR	EM / EX / BR	EM / EX / BR
_____	EM / EX / BR	EM / EX / BR	EM / EX / BR	EM / EX / BR	EM / EX / BR
_____	EM / EX / BR	EM / EX / BR	EM / EX / BR	EM / EX / BR	EM / EX / BR
_____	EM / EX / BR	EM / EX / BR	EM / EX / BR	EM / EX / BR	EM / EX / BR
_____	EM / EX / BR	EM / EX / BR	EM / EX / BR	EM / EX / BR	EM / EX / BR
_____	EM / EX / BR	EM / EX / BR	EM / EX / BR	EM / EX / BR	EM / EX / BR
_____	EM / EX / BR	EM / EX / BR	EM / EX / BR	EM / EX / BR	EM / EX / BR
_____	EM / EX / BR	EM / EX / BR	EM / EX / BR	EM / EX / BR	EM / EX / BR
_____	EM / EX / BR	EM / EX / BR	EM / EX / BR	EM / EX / BR	EM / EX / BR
_____	EM / EX / BR	EM / EX / BR	EM / EX / BR	EM / EX / BR	EM / EX / BR
_____	EM / EX / BR	EM / EX / BR	EM / EX / BR	EM / EX / BR	EM / EX / BR
_____	EM / EX / BR	EM / EX / BR	EM / EX / BR	EM / EX / BR	EM / EX / BR
_____	EM / EX / BR	EM / EX / BR	EM / EX / BR	EM / EX / BR	EM / EX / BR

Writing: *Write About an Experience*

Writing Practice #1

Name:

Directions: You are going to write a paragraph in English about your personal experience. Read the writing prompt below. Complete the graphic organizer below by answering the questions in the thought clouds with simple words and/or phrases.

WHERE?
(Where did this experience take place?)

WHEN?
(Time? Year? Month? Season? Age?)

WHAT?
(What happened? What was it?)

WHY?

???

WHO?
(Who was there?)

HOW?
(How did you feel?)

Writing Prompt: *Think about a time when you learned something new that you really enjoyed. What was it? Who or what did you learn it from? Why was it interesting? How did you feel?*

54

Writing Practice #1 - cont'd

Name: _____

Directions: Complete the graphic organizer below to help you organize your writing. You can use the sentence starters to help you.

Sentence Starters	BEGINNING *(What happened first?)*
• First, ... • One day ... • One time ... • One year ... • During ...	

Sentence Starters	MIDDLE *(What happened next?)*
• Then ... • After that ... • Later, ... • After ... • During ...	

Sentence Starters	END *(What happened last?)*
• Finally, ... • Last, ... • In the end, ... • At the end ... • So, ...	

Writing Prompt: *Think about a time when you learned something new that you really enjoyed. What was it? Who or what did you learn it from? Why was it interesting? How did you feel?*

Writing Practice #1 - cont'd

Name: _____

Directions: You are going to write your paragraph in the box below. Use the information in your graphic organizers to help you write.

Writing Prompt: Think about a time when you learned something new that you really enjoyed. What was it? Who or what did you learn it from? Why was it interesting? How did you feel?

Writing Practice #2

Name: ....

Directions: You are going to write a paragraph in English about your personal experience. Read the writing prompt below. Complete the graphic organizer below by answering the questions in the thought clouds with simple words and/or phrases.

WHERE?
(Where did this experience take place?)

WHEN?
(Time? Year? Month? Season? Age?)

WHAT?
(What happened? What was it?)

WHY?

WHO?
(Who was there?)

???

HOW?
(How did you feel?)

Writing Prompt: *Think about a time when you felt proud of something that you accomplished. What was it? How did you accomplish it? What did you learn from that experience?*

57

Writing Practice #2 - cont'd

Name: _____

Directions: Complete the graphic organizer below to help you organize your writing. You can use the sentence starters to help you.

Sentence Starters	**BEGINNING** *(What happened first?)*
• First, ... • One day ... • One time ... • One year ... • During ...	

Sentence Starters	**MIDDLE** *(What happened next?)*
• Then ... • After that ... • Later, ... • After ... • During ...	

Sentence Starters	**END** *(What happened last?)*
• Finally, ... • Last, ... • In the end, ... • At the end ... • So, ...	

Writing Prompt: *Think about a time when you felt proud of something that you accomplished. What was it? How did you accomplish it? What did you learn from that experience?*

Writing Practice #2 - cont'd

Name: _____

Directions: You are going to write your paragraph in the box below. Use the information in your graphic organizers to help you write.

Writing Prompt: Think about a time when you felt proud of something that you accomplished. What was it? How did you accomplish it? What did you learn from that experience?

_____

_____

_____

_____

_____

_____

_____

_____

_____

_____

_____

_____

_____

_____

_____

_____

_____

_____

_____

Writing Practice #3

Name: _____

Directions: You are going to write a paragraph in English about your personal experience. Read the writing prompt below. Complete the graphic organizer below by answering the questions in the thought clouds with simple words and/or phrases.

WHERE?
(Where did this experience take place?)

WHEN?
(Time? Year? Month? Season? Age?)

WHAT?
(What happened? What was it?)

WHY?

WHO?
(Who was there?)

???

HOW?
(How did you feel?)

Writing Prompt: *Think about a time when you felt brave even though it was a challenge. What happened? How did you overcome the challenge? What did you learn from that experience?*

Writing Practice #3 - cont'd

Name: ....

Directions: Complete the graphic organizer below to help you organize your writing. You can use the sentence starters to help you.

Sentence Starters	BEGINNING (What happened first?)
• First, ... • One day ... • One time ... • One year ... • During ...	

Sentence Starters	MIDDLE (What happened next?)
• Then ... • After that ... • Later, ... • After ... • During ...	

Sentence Starters	END (What happened last?)
• Finally, ... • Last, ... • In the end, ... • At the end ... • So, ...	

Writing Prompt: *Think about a time when you felt brave even though it was a challenge. What happened? How did you overcome the challenge? What did you learn from that experience?*

Writing Practice #3 - cont'd

Name:

Directions: You are going to write your paragraph in the box below. Use the information in your graphic organizers to help you write.

Writing Prompt: Think about a time when you felt brave even though it was a challenge. What happened? How did you overcome the challenge? What did you learn from that experience?

Writing Practice #4

Name: ....

Directions: You are going to write a paragraph in English about your personal experience. Read the writing prompt below. Complete the graphic organizer below by answering the questions in the thought clouds with simple words and/or phrases.

WHERE?
(Where did this experience take place?)

WHEN?
(Time? Year? Month? Season? Age?)

WHAT?
(What happened? What was it?)

WHY?

WHO?
(Who was there?)

HOW?
(How did you feel?)

Writing Prompt: *Think about a time when you did something nice for someone or someone did something nice for you. What was it? How did it make you feel? How do you think the other person felt? Why is it important to be nice and kind?*

Writing Practice #4 - cont'd

Name: _____

Directions: Complete the graphic organizer below to help you organize your writing. You can use the sentence starters to help you.

Sentence Starters	BEGINNING
• First, ... • One day ... • One time ... • One year ... • During ...	*(What happened first?)*

Sentence Starters	MIDDLE
• Then ... • After that ... • Later, ... • After ... • During ...	*(What happened next?)*

Sentence Starters	END
• Finally, ... • Last, ... • In the end, ... • At the end ... • So, ...	*(What happened last?)*

Writing Prompt: *Think about a time when you did something nice for someone or someone did something nice for you. What was it? How did it make you feel? How do you think the other person felt? Why is it important to be nice and kind?*

Writing Practice #4 - cont'd

Name:

Directions: You are going to write your paragraph in the box below. Use the information in your graphic organizers to help you write.

Writing Prompt: Think about a time when you did something nice for someone or someone did something nice for you. What was it? How did it make you feel? How do you think the other person felt? Why is it important to be nice and kind?

Writing Practice #5

Name: ....

Directions: You are going to write a paragraph in English about your personal experience. Read the writing prompt below. Complete the graphic organizer below by answering the questions in the thought clouds with simple words and/or phrases.

WHERE?
(Where did this experience take place?)

WHEN?
(Time? Year? Month? Season? Age?)

WHAT?
(What happened? What was it?)

WHY?

WHO?
(Who was there?)

HOW?
(How did you feel?)

Writing Prompt: *Think about a time when you were excited for a school activity or event. What was the activity or event? Why did you feel excited? What happened? What made the activity or event so memorable?*

Writing Practice #5 - cont'd

Name: _____

Directions: Complete the graphic organizer below to help you organize your writing. You can use the sentence starters to help you.

Sentence Starters	**BEGINNING** *(What happened first?)*
• First, ... • One day ... • One time ... • One year ... • During ...	

Sentence Starters	**MIDDLE** *(What happened next?)*
• Then ... • After that ... • Later, ... • After ... • During ...	

Sentence Starters	**END** *(What happened last?)*
• Finally, ... • Last, ... • In the end, ... • At the end ... • So, ...	

Writing Prompt: Think about a time when you were excited for a school activity or event. What was the activity or event? Why did you feel excited? What happened? What made the activity or event so memorable?

Writing Practice #5 - cont'd

Name: ....

Directions: You are going to write your paragraph in the box below. Use the information in your graphic organizers to help you write.

....

<u>Writing Prompt:</u> **Think about a time when you were excited for a school activity or event. What was the activity or event? Why did you feel excited? What happened? What made the activity or event so memorable?**

Writing Practice - *Blank Template*

Name: ....

Directions: You are going to write a paragraph in English about your personal experience. Read the writing prompt below. Complete the graphic organizer below by answering the questions in the thought clouds with simple words and/or phrases.

WHERE?
(Where did this experience take place?)

WHEN?
(Time? Year? Month? Season? Age?)

WHAT?
(What happened? What was it?)

WHY?

???

WHO?
(Who was there?)

HOW?
(How did you feel?)

Writing Prompt:

Writing Practice - *Blank Template*

Name: _____

Directions: Complete the graphic organizer below to help you organize your writing. You can use the sentence starters to help you.

Sentence Starters	BEGINNING *(What happened first?)*
• First, ... • One day ... • One time ... • One year ... • During ...	

Sentence Starters	MIDDLE *(What happened next?)*
• Then ... • After that ... • Later, ... • After ... • During ...	

Sentence Starters	END *(What happened last?)*
• Finally, ... • Last, ... • In the end, ... • At the end ... • So, ...	

Writing Prompt:

Writing Practice - *Blank Template*

Name: ....
_____

Directions: You are going to write your paragraph in the box below. Use the information in your graphic organizers to help you write.
....

Writing Prompt:

_____
_____
_____
_____
_____
_____
_____
_____
_____
_____
_____
_____
_____
_____
_____
_____
_____
_____

Writing
Write About Academic Information

This section includes:
- Guided Activities
- Teacher's ELD Standards Record Sheet
- Student Practice Activities:
  - Graphic Organizers
  - Academic information writing practice
  - Bonus blank writing template

Alignment to CA ELD Standards:	**Alignment to CCSS:**
Part I: Interacting in Meaningful Ways B.6 Reading/viewing closely Reading closely literary and informational texts and viewing multimedia to determine how meaning is conveyed explicitly and implicitly through language	RL.3.1–7,9–10; RI.3.1–7,9-10; SL.3.2–3; L.3.3, 4, 6 RL.4.1–7, 9–10; RI.4.1–7, 9–10; SL.4.2–3; L.4.3, 4, 6 RL.5.1–7, 9–10; RI.5.1–7, 9–10; SL.5.2–3; L.5.3, 4, 6
Part I: Interacting in Meaningful Ways C.11 Supporting Opinions Supporting own opinions and evaluating others' opinions in speaking and writing	W.3.1, 4, 10; SL.3.4, 6; L.3.1–3, 6 W.4.1, 4, 9–10; SL.4.4, 6; L.4.1–3, 6 W.5.1, 4, 9–10; SL.5.4, 6; L.5.1–3, 6
Part I: Interacting in Meaningful Ways C.12 Selecting Language Resources Selecting and applying varied and precise vocabulary and language structures to effectively convey ideas	W.3.4–5; SL.3.4, 6; L.3.1, 3, 5–6 W.4.4–5; SL.4.4, 6; L.4.1, 3, 5–6 W.5.4–5; SL.5.4, 6; L.5.1, 3, 5–6
Part II: Learning About How English Works B.3 Expanding and Enriching Ideas Using verbs and verb phrases	W.3.5; SL.3.6; L.3.1, 3, 6 W.4.5; SL.4.6; L.4.1, 3, 6 W.5.5; SL.5.6; L.5.1, 3, 6
Part II: Learning About How English Works B.4 Expanding and Enriching Ideas Using nouns and noun phrases	W.3.5; SL.3.6; L.3.1, 3, 6 W.4.5; SL.4.6; L.4.1, 3, 6 W.5.5; SL.5.6; L.5.1, 3, 6
Part II: Learning About How English Works B.5 Expanding and Enriching Ideas Modifying to add details	W.3.5; SL.3.4, 6; L.3.1, 3, 6 W.4.5; SL.4.4, 6; L.4.1, 3, 6 W.5.5; SL.5.4, 6; L.5.1, 3, 6

Writing
Write About Academic Information

- -

Alignment to CA ELD Standards:

Part II: Learning About How English Works
  C.6 Connecting and Condensing Ideas
  Connecting ideas

Part II: Learning About How English Works
  C.7 Connecting and Condensing Ideas
  Condensing ideas

Alignment to CCSS:

W.3.1-3, 5; SL.3.4, 6; L.3.1, 3, 6
W.4.1–3, 5; SL.4.4, 6; L.4.1, 3, 6
W.5.1–3, 5; SL.5.4, 6; L.5.1, 3, 6

W.3.1-3, 5; SL.3.4, 6; L.3.1, 3, 6
W.4.1–3, 5; SL.4.4, 6; L.4.1, 3, 6
W.5.1–3, 5; SL.5.4, 6; L.5.1, 3, 6

- -

Guided Activities Direction:

1. Show students the graphic organizer and writing questions.
2. Guide students in reading and understanding the academic information in the graphic organizer as if it was completed by a peer.
3. Guide students through:
   - Reading and comprehending academic information and details
   - Identifying the parts of the graphic organizer
   - Writing sentences using relevant details from the graphic organizer
4. Then have students practice with additional writing activities for academic information.

Guided Activity #1

Name: _____

Directions: You are writing a description with a classmate. Your classmate filled in the information about Bottlenose Dolphins. Look at the details. Then you will write more of the description.

Appearance
- 6-12 feet long
- gray color
- blowhole on top of head
- tail, dorsal fin, and flippers

Animal

Bottlenose Dolphin
(mammals)

Habitat
- ocean
- warm waters
- some live in shallow waters
- some live in deep waters

Diet
- small fish
- squid
- shrimp

Behavior Traits
- intelligent
- good eyesight and hearing
- use echolocation (high-clicking sounds to navigate)

1 Your classmate started writing the description with this sentence:

Bottlenose Dolphins are mammals that can grow six to twelve feet long.

Now it's your turn to add to the description. Write one sentence telling more about the appearance. Use the details from your classmate to help you.

_____

_____

_____

2 Now continue describing Bottlenose Dolphins. Write two or more sentences providing additional information about their habitat, diet, and behavior traits. Use the details from your classmate to help you.

_____

_____

_____

_____

_____

Guided Activity #2

Name:

Directions: You are writing a description with a classmate. Your classmate filled in the information about tornados. Look at the details. Then you will write more of the description.

Characteristics	Cause
• fast spinning vortex of air • touches the ground • high winds • heavy rain	• occurs during thunderstorms • high humidity • strong winds going in opposite directions

Weather

tornado
(twister)

Effects	Safety
• heavy wind damage • destroy homes and cars • path of destruction • topple trees and poles	• tornado warnings • evacuate the area • find shelter • stay away from windows

1 Your classmate started writing the description with this sentence:

Tornados are dangerous weather systems characterized by a fast spinning vortex of air.

Now it's your turn to add to the description. Write one sentence telling more about the characteristic. Use the details from your classmate to help you.

_____

_____

_____

_____

2 Now continue describing tornados. Write two or more sentences providing additional information about the cause, effects, and safety. Use the details from your classmate to help you.

_____

_____

_____

_____

_____

_____

Guided Activity #3

Name: _____

Directions: You are writing a description with a classmate. Your classmate filled in the information about Venus flytraps. Look at the details. Then you will write more of the description.

Appearance
- small plant
- clam-shaped leaves
- stiff hairs on edges of leaves
- red inside of leaves

Plant

Venus flytrap
(carnivorous)

Habitat
- North America
- North and South Carolina
- marshy areas
- moist, acidic soils

Diet
- moths
- ants
- flies
- grasshoppers

Interesting facts
- a plant that eats insects
- attracts insects with sweet smell
- snaps shut and digests an insect when hairs on leaves are triggered

1 Your classmate started writing the description with this sentence:

A Venus flytrap is a carnivorous plant that has clam-shaped leaves.

Now it's your turn to add to the description. Write one sentence telling more about the appearance. Use the details from your classmate to help you.

_____

_____

_____

2 Now continue describing Venus flytraps. Write two or more sentences providing additional information about the habitat, diet, and interesting facts. Use the details from your classmate to help you.

_____

_____

_____

_____

_____

Guided Activity #4

Name: _____

Directions: You are writing a description with a classmate. Your classmate filled in the information about chameleons. Look at the details. Then you will write more of the description.

Appearance
- pair of eyes that move independently of each other
- long, sticky tongues
- long tails

Habitat
- Africa, Southeast Asia, Spain
- rainforests and deserts
- in trees
- on the ground

Animal

chameleon *(reptile)*

Diet
- insects
- small birds
- other small lizards

Interesting Facts
- can change color/camouflage
- one of world's fastest muscle movements in their tongues
- over 160 species

1 Your classmate started writing the description with this sentence:
A chameleon is a reptile that has a pair of eyes that can move independently of each other.
Now it's your turn to add to the description. Write one sentence telling more about the appearance. Use the details from your classmate to help you.

_____

_____

_____

_____

2 Now continue describing chameleons. Write two or more sentences providing additional information about the habitat, diet, and interesting facts. Use the details from your classmate to help you.

_____

_____

_____

_____

_____

_____

Guided Activity #5

Name: _____

Directions: You are writing a description with a classmate. Your classmate filled in the information about Jupiter. Look at the details. Then you will write more of the description.

Appearance
- colorful bands of clouds and spots
- three distinct layers
- white, shades of browns, and orange

Composition
- mostly hydrogen and helium
- thick clouds of ammonia and water vapor
- no solid surface

Planets

Jupiter
(gas giant)

Size & Distance
- largest planet in solar system
- diameter of 86,881 miles
- distance from sun = 483.8 million miles

Unique Features
- Giant Red Spot (hurricane)
- powerful gravitational pull
- has 79 moons
- a day on Jupiter is just 10 hours

1 Your classmate started writing the description with this sentence:
Jupiter is a gas giant planet that has colorful bands of clouds and spots.

Now it's your turn to add to the description. Write one sentence telling more about the appearance. Use the details from your classmate to help you.

_____

_____

_____

2 Now continue describing Jupiter. Write two or more sentences providing additional information about the composition, size, distance, and unique features. Use the details from your classmate to help you.

_____

_____

_____

_____

_____

ELD Standards Record Sheet

Directions:

1. Look at the CA ELD standards (**BELOW**) that correspond to this section.
2. Reference these specific standards for the template Record Sheet.
3. Use the following template Record Sheet to monitor students' proficiency levels for the **GUIDED ACTIVITIES** in this section.
4. Fill out all the information. Circle, check, highlight the proficiency level. (*There is space for 20 students. Make additional copies, as needed*)
5. Retain for your records to be used during grading, parent/student conferences, lesson planning, ELD documentation, etc.

Suggestion: You can make one copy of each guided activity and/or the student practice sheets and laminate them. Organize the laminated sheets onto a book ring. Now it'll be easily accessible for whole group, small group, one-on-one, centers, etc. Copy as many of the ELD Standards Record Sheet as you need and keep it handy along with the activities.

ELD Standards Record Sheet

CA ELD Standards & Proficiency Levels
Part I: Interacting in Meaningful Ways
B.6 Reading/Viewing Closely

EMERGING (EM)	EXPANDING (EX)	BRIDGING (BR)
Requires **Substantial** Support	Requires **Moderate** Support	Requires **Light** Support

GRADE 3

• Describes:
  ◦ Ideas
  ◦ phenomena (e.g., insect metamorphosis)
  ◦ text elements (e.g. main idea, characters, setting)
• Reads and comprehends a select set of grade-level texts and multimedia with:
  ◦ Simple sentences
  ◦ Familiar vocabulary
  ◦ Support by graphics or pictures
• Requires substantial support
	• Describes in greater details:
	  ◦ Ideas
	  ◦ Phenomena (e.g., how cows digest food)
	  ◦ text elements (e.g. main idea, characters, events)
	• Reads and comprehends a <u>variety of</u> grade-level texts and multimedia with:
	  ◦ <u>Reliance on content and prior knowledge to obtain meaning from print</u>
	  ◦ Support by graphics or pictures
	• Requires <u>moderate</u> support
		• Describes using key details:
		  ◦ Ideas
		  ◦ phenomena (e.g., volcanic eruptions)
		  ◦ text elements (e.g. central message, character traits, major events)
		• Reads and comprehends a variety of grade-level texts and multimedia with:
		  ◦ <u>Limited comprehension difficulty</u>
		  ◦ <u>Comprehension of concrete and abstract topics</u>
		  ◦ <u>Recognize language subtleties</u>
		  ◦ Support by graphics or pictures
		• Requires <u>light</u> support

GRADE 4

• Describes:
  ◦ Ideas
  ◦ phenomena (e.g., volcanic eruptions)
  ◦ text elements (e.g. main idea, characters, setting)
• Based on close reading of a select set of grade-level texts
• Requires substantial support
• Use knowledge of frequently-used affixes (e.g. un-, mis-) and linguistic context, reference materials, and visual cues to:
  ◦ Determine the meaning of unknown words on familiar topics
	• Describes in <u>greater</u> details:
	  ◦ Ideas
	  ◦ phenomena (e.g., animal migration)
	  ◦ text elements (e.g. main idea, central message, etc)
	• Based on close reading of a <u>variety of</u> grade-level texts
	• Requires <u>moderate</u> support
	• Use knowledge of <u>morphology (e.g. affixes, roots, and base words)</u> and linguistic context, reference materials, and visual cues to:
	  ◦ Determine the meaning of unknown words on familiar topics
		• Describes <u>in detail:</u>
		  ◦ Ideas
		  ◦ phenomena (e.g., pollination)
		  ◦ text elements (e.g. main idea, character traits, event sequence, etc.)
		• Based on close reading of a variety of grade-level texts
		• Requires <u>light</u> support
		• Use knowledge of morphology (e.g. affixes, roots, and base words) and linguistic context to:
		  ◦ Determine the meaning of unknown and <u>multiple-meaning words</u> on familiar and <u>new</u> topics

GRADE 5

• Explain:
  ◦ Ideas
  ◦ phenomena
  ◦ text relationships (e.g.compare/contrastcause/effect, problem/solution)
• Based on close reading of a variety of grade-level texts and viewing of multimedia
• Requires substantial support
• Use knowledge of frequently-used affixes (e.g. un-, mis-) linguistic context, reference materials, and visual cues to:
  ◦ Determine the meaning of unknown words on familiar topics
	• Explain:
	  ◦ Ideas
	  ◦ Phenomena
	  ◦ <u>processes</u>
	  ◦ text relationships (e.g. compare/contrast, cause/effect, problem/solution)
	• Based on close reading of a variety of grade-level texts and viewing of multimedia
	• Requires <u>moderate</u> support
	• Use knowledge of <u>morphology (e.g. affixes, roots, and base words)</u> linguistic context, reference materials to:
	  ◦ Determine the meaning of unknown words on familiar and <u>new</u> topics
		• Explain:
		  ◦ Ideas
		  ◦ Phenomena
		  ◦ processes
		  ◦ text relationships (e.g. compare/contrast, cause/ effect, problem/ solution)
		• Based on close reading of a variety of grade-level texts and viewing of multimedia
		• Requires <u>light</u> support
		• Use knowledge of morphology (e.g. affixes, roots, and base words), linguistic context, and reference materials to:
		  ◦ Determine the meaning of unknown words on familiar and new topics

ELD Standards Record Sheet

CA ELD Standards & Proficiency Levels
Part I: Interacting in Meaningful Ways
C.11 Supporting Opinions

EMERGING (EM)	EXPANDING (EX)	BRIDGING (BR)
*Requires **Substantial** Support*	*Requires **Moderate** Support*	*Requires **Light** Support*
GRADE 3		

• Support opinions by providing:
   ◦ good reasons
   ◦ some textual evidence
   ◦ relevant background knowledge (e.g. referring to textual evidence or knowledge of content)
	• Support opinions by providing:
	   ◦ good reasons
	   ◦ <u>increasingly detailed</u> textual evidence
	   ◦ relevant background knowledge <u>about the content</u> (e.g. providing examples from the text)
		• Support opinions or <u>persuade others</u> by providing:
		   ◦ good reasons
		   ◦ <u>detailed</u> textual evidence
		   ◦ relevant background knowledge about the content (e.g. specific evidence or graphics from text)

GRADE 4		

• Support opinions by expressing appropriate/accurate reasons using:
   ◦ textual evidence (e.g. referring to text)
   ◦ relevant background knowledge about content
• Requires substantial support
• Express ideas and opinions or expressions (e.g. can, will, maybe)
	• Support opinions or <u>persuade others</u> by expressing appropriate/accurate reasons using:
	   ◦ <u>Some</u> textual evidence (e.g. Paraphrasing facts)
	   ◦ relevant background knowledge about content
	   ◦ Requires <u>moderate</u> support
	   ◦ Express <u>attitude</u> and opinions or <u>temper statements with familiar modal</u> expressions (e.g. maybe/probably, can/must)
		• Support opinions or persuade others by expressing appropriate/accurate reasons using:
		   ◦ <u>Detailed</u> textual evidence (e.g. Quotations or specific events from text)
		   ◦ relevant background knowledge about content
		• Requires <u>light</u> support
		• Express attitude and opinions or temper statements with <u>nuanced modal</u> expressions (e.g. probably/certainly, should/would) and paraphrasing (e.g. In my opinion…)

GRADE 5		

• Support opinions by expressing appropriate/accurate reasons using:
   ◦ textual evidence (e.g. referring to text)
   ◦ relevant background knowledge about content
• Requires substantial support
• Express ideas and opinions or expressions (e.g. can, will, maybe)
	• Support opinions or <u>persuade others</u> by expressing appropriate/accurate reasons using:
	   ◦ <u>Some</u> textual evidence (e.g. paraphrasing facts)
	   ◦ relevant background knowledge about content
	• Requires <u>moderate</u> support
	• Express <u>attitude</u> and opinions or <u>temper statements with familiar modal</u> expressions (e.g. maybe/probably, can/must)
		• Support opinions or persuade others by expressing appropriate/accurate reasons using:
		   ◦ <u>Detailed</u> textual evidence (e.g. Quotations or specific events from text)
		   ◦ relevant background knowledge about content
		• Requires <u>light</u> support
		• Express attitude and opinions or temper statements with <u>nuanced modal</u> expressions (e.g. probably/certainly, should/would) and paraphrasing (e.g. In my opinion…)

ELD Standards Record Sheet

CA ELD Standards & Proficiency Levels
Part I: Interacting in Meaningful Ways
C.12 Selecting Language Resources

EMERGING (EM)	EXPANDING (EX)	BRIDGING (BR)
*Requires **Substantial** Support*	*Requires **Moderate** Support*	*Requires **Light** Support*
GRADE 3		
• Use a select number of general academic and domain-specific words: ◦ to add detail (e.g. adding the word dangerous to describe a place, using the word habitat when describing animal behavior) • Uses the words while speaking and writing	• Use a growing number of general academic and domain-specific words in order to: ◦ add detail ◦ create an effect (e.g. using the word suddenly to signal a change) ◦ create shades of meaning (e.g.scurry vs. dash) • Uses the words while speaking and writing	• Use a wide variety of general academic and domain-specific words , synonyms, antonyms, and non-literal language to: ◦ create an effect ◦ precision ◦ shades of meaning • Uses the words while speaking and writing
GRADE 4		
• Use a select number of general academic and domain-specific words to create precision while speaking and writing • Select a few frequently used affixes for accuracy and precision (e.g. She walks, I'm unhappy.)	• Use a growing number of general academic and domain-specific words, synonyms, and antonyms to create precision and shades of meaning while speaking and writing • Select a growing number of frequently used affixes for accuracy and precision (e.g. She walked. He likes…, I'm unhappy.)	• Use a wide variety number of general academic and domain-specific words, synonyms, and antonyms, and figurative language to create precision and shades of meaning while speaking and writing • Select a variety of appropriate affixes for accuracy and precision (e.g. She walking. I'm uncomfortable. They left reluctantly.)
GRADE 5		
• Use a select number of general academic and domain-specific words to create precision while speaking and writing • Select a few frequently used affixes for accuracy and precision (e.g. She walks, I'm unhappy.)	• Use a growing number of general academic and domain-specific words, synonyms, and antonyms to create precision and shades of meaning while speaking and writing • Select a growing number of frequently used affixes for accuracy and precision (e.g. She walked. He likes…, I'm unhappy.)	• Use a wide variety number of general academic and domain-specific words, synonyms, and antonyms, and figurative language to create precision and shades of meaning while speaking and writing • Select a variety of appropriate affixes for accuracy and precision (e.g. She walking. I'm uncomfortable. They left reluctantly.)

Writing: *Write About Academic Information*

ELD Standards Record Sheet

CA ELD Standards & Proficiency Levels

Part II: Learning About How English Works
B.3 Using Verbs and Verb Phrases

EMERGING (EM)	EXPANDING (EX)	BRIDGING (BR)
Requires **Substantial** Support	Requires **Moderate** Support	Requires **Light** Support
GRADE 3		
• Use frequently used verbs • Use different verb types (e.g. doing, saying, being/having, thinking/feeling) • Use different verb tenses (e.g. simple past for recounting an experience) • Appropriate for the text type and discipline to convey time	• Use a <u>growing number</u> of verb types (e.g. doing, saying, being/having, thinking/feeling) • Use a <u>growing number</u> of verb tenses (e.g. simple past for retelling, simple present for a science description) • Appropriate for the text type and discipline to convey time	• Use a <u>variety</u> of verb types (e.g. doing, saying, being/having, thinking/feeling) • Use a <u>variety</u> of verb tenses (e.g. simple present for a science description, simple future to predict) • Appropriate for the text type and discipline to convey time
GRADE 4		
• Use various verbs • Use various verb types (e.g. doing, saying, being/having, thinking/feeling) • Use various verb tenses (e.g. simple past for recounting an experience) • Appropriate for the text type and discipline for familiar topics	• Use various verbs • Use various verb types (e.g. doing, saying, being/having, thinking/feeling) • Use various verb tenses (e.g. simple past for retelling, timeless present for science explanation) • Appropriate for the <u>task</u>, text type and discipline • <u>For an increasing variety of familiar and new topics</u>	• Use various verb • Use various verb types (e.g. doing, saying, being/having, thinking/feeling) • Use various verb tenses(e.g. timeless present for science explanation, mixture of past and present for historical information report) • Appropriate for the task and text type • For a <u>variety</u> of familiar and new topics
GRADE 5		
• Use frequently used verbs (e.g. take, like, eat) • Use various verb types (e.g. doing, saying, being/having, thinking/feeling) • Use various verb tenses (e.g. simple past for recounting an experience) • Appropriate for the text type and discipline for familiar topics	• Use <u>various</u> verb types (e.g. doing, saying, being/having, thinking/feeling) • Use various verb tenses (e.g. simple past for retelling, timeless present for science a description) • Appropriate for the <u>task</u>, text type and discipline • <u>For an increasing variety of topics</u>	• Use various verb types (e.g. doing, saying, being/having, thinking/feeling) • Use various verb tenses (e.g. timeless present for science description, mixture of past and present for narrative or history explanation) • Appropriate for the task and text type • For a <u>variety</u> of topics

Writing: *Write About Academic Information*

ELD Standards Record Sheet

CA ELD Standards & Proficiency Levels

Part II: Learning About How English Works
B.4 Using Nouns and Noun Phrases

EMERGING (EM)	EXPANDING (EX)	BRIDGING (BR)
*Requires **Substantial** Support*	*Requires **Moderate** Support*	*Requires **Light** Support*
GRADE 3		
• *Expand noun phrases in simple ways in order to enrich:* 　○ *The meaning of sentences* 　○ *Add details about ideas, people, things, etc. (e.g. adding an adjective to a noun)*	• *Expand noun phrases in a <u>growing number</u> of ways in order to enrich:* 　○ *The meaning of sentences* 　○ *Add details about ideas, people, things, etc. (e.g. adding comparative/superlative adjectives to nouns)*	• *Expand noun phrases in a <u>variety</u> of ways in order to enrich:* 　○ *The meaning of sentences and* 　○ *Add details about ideas, people, things, etc. (e.g. adding comparative/superlative adjectives to nouns, simple clause embedding)*
GRADE 4		
• *Expand noun phrases in simple ways in order to enrich:* 　○ *The meaning of sentences* 　○ *Add details about ideas, people, things, etc. (e.g. adding an adjective)*	• *Expand noun phrases in a <u>variety</u> of ways in order to enrich:* 　○ *The meaning of sentences* 　○ *Add details about ideas, people, things, etc. (e.g. adding adjectives to noun phrases or simple clause embedding)*	• *Expand noun phrases in an <u>increasing variety</u> of ways in order to enrich:* 　○ *The meaning of sentences and* 　○ *Add details about ideas, people, things, etc. (e.g. adding general academic adjectives and adverbs to noun phrases or more complex clause embedding)*
GRADE 5		
• *Expand noun phrases in simple ways in order to enrich:* 　○ *The meaning of sentences* 　○ *Add details about ideas, people, things, etc. (e.g. adding an adjective to a noun)*	• *Expand noun phrases in a <u>variety</u> of ways in order to enrich:* 　○ *The meaning of sentences* 　○ *Add details about ideas, people, things, etc. (e.g. adding comparative/superlative adjectives to noun phrases or simple clause embedding)*	• *Expand noun phrases in an <u>increasing variety</u> of ways in order to enrich:* 　○ *The meaning of sentences* 　○ *Add details about ideas, people, things, etc. (e.g. adding comparative/superlative and general academic adjectives to noun phrases or more complex clause embedding)*

ELD Standards Record Sheet

CA ELD Standards & Proficiency Levels
Part II: Learning About How English Works
B.5 Modifying to Add Details

EMERGING (EM)→	→EXPANDING (EX)→	→BRIDGING (BR)
*Requires **Substantial** Support*	*Requires **Moderate** Support*	*Requires **Light** Support*
GRADE 3		
• *Expand sentences with adverbials (e.g. adverbs, adverb phrases, prepositional phrases)* • *Use these to provide details about a familiar activity or process (e.g. time, manner, place, cause) (e.g. They walked to the soccer field.)*	• *Expand sentences with adverbials (e.g. adverbs, adverb phrases, prepositional phrases)* • *Use these to provide details about a familiar or <u>new activity</u> or process (e.g. time, manner, place, cause) (e.g. They worked quietly; They ran across the soccer field.)*	• *Expand sentences with adverbials (e.g. adverbs, adverb phrases, prepositional phrases)* • *Use these to provide details about a <u>range</u> of familiar and new activities or processes.(e.g. time, manner, place, cause) (e.g. They worked quietly all night in their room.)*
GRADE 4		
• *Expand sentences with familiar adverbials (e.g. basic prepositional phrases)* • *Use these to provide details about a familiar activity or process (e.g. time, manner, place, cause) (e.g. They walked to the soccer field.)*	• *Expand sentences with a <u>growing variety</u> of adverbials (e.g. adverbs, prepositional phrases)* • *Use these to provide details about a familiar or <u>new activity</u> or process (e.g. time, manner, place, cause) (e.g. They worked quietly; They ran across the soccer field.)*	• *Expand sentences with a <u>variety</u> of adverbials (e.g. adverbs, adverb phrases, prepositional phrases)* • *Use these to provide details about a <u>variety</u> of familiar and new activities or processes.(e.g. time, manner, place, cause) (e.g. They worked quietly all night in their room.)*
GRADE 5		
• *Expand and enrich sentences with adverbials (e.g. adverbs, adverb phrases, prepositional phrases)* • *Use these to provide details about a familiar activity or process (e.g. time, manner, place, cause)*	• *Expand and enrich sentences with adverbials (e.g. adverbs, adverb phrases, prepositional phrases)* • *Use these to provide details about a familiar or <u>new activity</u> or process (e.g. time, manner, place, cause)*	• *Expand and enrich sentences with adverbials (e.g. adverbs, adverb phrases, prepositional phrases)* • *Use these to provide details about a <u>variety</u> of familiar and new activities or processes.(e.g. time, manner, place, cause)*

ELD Standards Record Sheet

CA ELD Standards & Proficiency Levels
Part II: Learning About How English Works
C.6 Connecting Ideas

EMERGING (EM)	EXPANDING (EX)	BRIDGING (BR)
Requires **Substantial** Support	Requires **Moderate** Support	Requires **Light** Support

GRADE 3

EMERGING (EM)	EXPANDING (EX)	BRIDGING (BR)
• Combine clauses in a few basic ways • To make connections between and to join ideas (e.g. creating compound sentences using and, but, so)	• Combine clauses in an _increasing variety_ of ways (e.g. creating compound and complex sentences) • to make connections between and to join ideas, for example: 　◦ _to express cause/effect (e.g. The deer ran because the mountain lion came.)_ 　◦ _to make a concession (e.g. She studied all night even though she wasn't feeling well.)_	• Combine clauses in a _wide variety_ of ways (e.g. creating compound and complex sentences) • to make connections between and to join ideas, for example: 　◦ to express cause/effect (e.g. The deer ran because the mountain lion approached them.) 　◦ to make a concession(e.g. She studied all night even though she wasn't feeling well.) 　◦ _to link two ideas that happen at the same time (e.g. The cubs played while their mother hunted.)_

GRADE 4

EMERGING (EM)	EXPANDING (EX)	BRIDGING (BR)
• Combine clauses in a few basic ways • To make connections between and to join ideas in sentences (e.g. creating compound sentences using coordinate conjunctions, such as and, but, so)	• Combine clauses in an _increasing variety_ of ways (e.g. creating complex sentences using familiar subordinate conjunctions) • to make connections between and to join ideas in sentences, for example: 　◦ _to express cause/effect (e.g. The deer ran because the mountain lion came.)_ 　◦ _to make a concession (e.g. She studied all night even though she wasn't feeling well.)_	• Combine clauses in a _wide variety_ of ways (e.g. creating complex sentences using a variety of subordinate conjunctions) • to make connections between and to join ideas, for example: 　◦ to express cause/effect (e.g. Since the lion was at the waterhole, the deer ran away.) 　◦ to make a concession 　◦ _to link two ideas that happen at the same time (e.g. The cubs played while their mother hunted.)_

GRADE 5

EMERGING (EM)	EXPANDING (EX)	BRIDGING (BR)
• Combine clauses in a few basic ways • To make connections between and to join ideas • To provide evidence to support ideas or opinions (e.g. You must X because X.) (e.g. creating compound sentences using and, but, so)	• Combine clauses in an _increasing variety_ of ways (e.g. creating compound and complex sentences) • to make connections between and to join ideas, for example: 　◦ _to express cause/effect (e.g. The deer ran because the mountain lion came.)_ 　◦ _to make a concession(e.g. She studied all night even though she wasn't feeling well.)_ • To provide reasons to support ideas (e.g. X is an extremely good book because X)	• Combine clauses in a _wide variety_ of ways (e.g. creating compound and complex sentences) • to make connections between and to join ideas, for example: 　◦ to express cause/effect (e.g. The deer ran because the mountain lion approached them.) 　◦ to make a concession (e.g. She studied all night even though she wasn't feeling well.) 　◦ _to link two ideas that happen at the same time (e.g. The cubs played while their mother hunted.)_ • To provide reasons to support ideas (e.g The author persuades the reader by X.)

Writing: *Write About Academic Information*

ELD Standards Record Sheet

CA ELD Standards & Proficiency Levels

Part II: Learning About How English Works
C.7 Condensing Ideas

EMERGING (EM)	EXPANDING (EX)	BRIDGING (BR)
Requires **Substantial** Support	Requires **Moderate** Support	Requires **Light** Support
GRADE 3		
• Condense clauses in simple ways to create precise and detailed sentences (e.g. It's green. It's red. It's green and red.)	• Condense clauses in a <u>growing number</u> of ways to create precise and detailed sentences (e.g. through embedded clauses as in, It's a plant. It's found in the rainforest. It's a green and red plant that's found in the tropical rainforest.)	• Condense clauses in a <u>variety of ways</u> to create precise and detailed sentences (e.g. through embedded clauses and other condensing, as in, It's a plant. It's green and red. It's found in the tropical rainforest. It's a green and red plant that's found in the tropical rainforest.)
GRADE 4		
• Condense clauses in simple ways to create precise and detailed sentences (e.g through simple embedded clauses as in, The woman is a doctor. She helps children. The woman is a doctor who helps children.)	• Condense clauses in an <u>increasing variety of ways</u> to create precise and detailed sentences (e.g. through a growing number of embedded clauses and other condensing as in, The dog ate quickly. The dog choked. The dog ate so quickly that it choked.)	• Condense clauses in a <u>variety of ways</u> to create precise and detailed sentences (e.g. through various types of embedded clauses and other ways of condensing, as in, There was a Gold Rush. It began in the 1850s. It brought a lot of people to California. The Gold Rush that began in the 1850s brought a lot of people to California.)
GRADE 5		
• Condense clauses in simple ways to create precise and detailed sentences (e.g through simple embedded clauses as in, The book is on the desk. The book is mine. The book that is on the desk is mine.)	• Condense clauses in an <u>increasing variety of ways</u> to create precise and detailed sentences (e.g. through a growing number of types of embedded clauses and other condensing as in, The book is mine. The book is about science. The book is on the desk. The science book that's on the desk is mine.)	• Condense clauses in a <u>variety of ways</u> to create precise and detailed sentences (e.g. through various types of embedded clauses and some nominalizations, as in, They were a very strong army. They had a lot of enemies. They crushed their enemies because they were strong. Their strength helped them crush their numerous enemies.)

87

ELD Standards Record Sheet

Teacher: _____ **Class:** _____

Standards: *PI.B.6*

Guided Activities and Proficiency Levels:

Students:	#1	#2	#3	#4	#5
_____	EM / EX / BR	EM / EX / BR	EM / EX / BR	EM / EX / BR	EM / EX / BR
_____	EM / EX / BR	EM / EX / BR	EM / EX / BR	EM / EX / BR	EM / EX / BR
_____	EM / EX / BR	EM / EX / BR	EM / EX / BR	EM / EX / BR	EM / EX / BR
_____	EM / EX / BR	EM / EX / BR	EM / EX / BR	EM / EX / BR	EM / EX / BR
_____	EM / EX / BR	EM / EX / BR	EM / EX / BR	EM / EX / BR	EM / EX / BR
_____	EM / EX / BR	EM / EX / BR	EM / EX / BR	EM / EX / BR	EM / EX / BR
_____	EM / EX / BR	EM / EX / BR	EM / EX / BR	EM / EX / BR	EM / EX / BR
_____	EM / EX / BR	EM / EX / BR	EM / EX / BR	EM / EX / BR	EM / EX / BR
_____	EM / EX / BR	EM / EX / BR	EM / EX / BR	EM / EX / BR	EM / EX / BR
_____	EM / EX / BR	EM / EX / BR	EM / EX / BR	EM / EX / BR	EM / EX / BR
_____	EM / EX / BR	EM / EX / BR	EM / EX / BR	EM / EX / BR	EM / EX / BR
_____	EM / EX / BR	EM / EX / BR	EM / EX / BR	EM / EX / BR	EM / EX / BR
_____	EM / EX / BR	EM / EX / BR	EM / EX / BR	EM / EX / BR	EM / EX / BR
_____	EM / EX / BR	EM / EX / BR	EM / EX / BR	EM / EX / BR	EM / EX / BR
_____	EM / EX / BR	EM / EX / BR	EM / EX / BR	EM / EX / BR	EM / EX / BR
_____	EM / EX / BR	EM / EX / BR	EM / EX / BR	EM / EX / BR	EM / EX / BR
_____	EM / EX / BR	EM / EX / BR	EM / EX / BR	EM / EX / BR	EM / EX / BR
_____	EM / EX / BR	EM / EX / BR	EM / EX / BR	EM / EX / BR	EM / EX / BR
_____	EM / EX / BR	EM / EX / BR	EM / EX / BR	EM / EX / BR	EM / EX / BR

ELD Standards Record Sheet

Teacher: _____ **Class:** _____

Standards: *PI.C.11*

Guided Activities and Proficiency Levels:

Students:	#1	#2	#3	#4	#5
_____	EM / EX / BR	EM / EX / BR	EM / EX / BR	EM / EX / BR	EM / EX / BR
_____	EM / EX / BR	EM / EX / BR	EM / EX / BR	EM / EX / BR	EM / EX / BR
_____	EM / EX / BR	EM / EX / BR	EM / EX / BR	EM / EX / BR	EM / EX / BR
_____	EM / EX / BR	EM / EX / BR	EM / EX / BR	EM / EX / BR	EM / EX / BR
_____	EM / EX / BR	EM / EX / BR	EM / EX / BR	EM / EX / BR	EM / EX / BR
_____	EM / EX / BR	EM / EX / BR	EM / EX / BR	EM / EX / BR	EM / EX / BR
_____	EM / EX / BR	EM / EX / BR	EM / EX / BR	EM / EX / BR	EM / EX / BR
_____	EM / EX / BR	EM / EX / BR	EM / EX / BR	EM / EX / BR	EM / EX / BR
_____	EM / EX / BR	EM / EX / BR	EM / EX / BR	EM / EX / BR	EM / EX / BR
_____	EM / EX / BR	EM / EX / BR	EM / EX / BR	EM / EX / BR	EM / EX / BR
_____	EM / EX / BR	EM / EX / BR	EM / EX / BR	EM / EX / BR	EM / EX / BR
_____	EM / EX / BR	EM / EX / BR	EM / EX / BR	EM / EX / BR	EM / EX / BR
_____	EM / EX / BR	EM / EX / BR	EM / EX / BR	EM / EX / BR	EM / EX / BR
_____	EM / EX / BR	EM / EX / BR	EM / EX / BR	EM / EX / BR	EM / EX / BR
_____	EM / EX / BR	EM / EX / BR	EM / EX / BR	EM / EX / BR	EM / EX / BR
_____	EM / EX / BR	EM / EX / BR	EM / EX / BR	EM / EX / BR	EM / EX / BR
_____	EM / EX / BR	EM / EX / BR	EM / EX / BR	EM / EX / BR	EM / EX / BR
_____	EM / EX / BR	EM / EX / BR	EM / EX / BR	EM / EX / BR	EM / EX / BR
_____	EM / EX / BR	EM / EX / BR	EM / EX / BR	EM / EX / BR	EM / EX / BR
_____	EM / EX / BR	EM / EX / BR	EM / EX / BR	EM / EX / BR	EM / EX / BR

ELD Standards Record Sheet

Teacher: _____ **Class:** _____

Standards: *PI.C.12*   **Guided Activities and Proficiency Levels:**

Students:	#1	#2	#3	#4	#5
_____	EM / EX / BR	EM / EX / BR	EM / EX / BR	EM / EX / BR	EM / EX / BR
_____	EM / EX / BR	EM / EX / BR	EM / EX / BR	EM / EX / BR	EM / EX / BR
_____	EM / EX / BR	EM / EX / BR	EM / EX / BR	EM / EX / BR	EM / EX / BR
_____	EM / EX / BR	EM / EX / BR	EM / EX / BR	EM / EX / BR	EM / EX / BR
_____	EM / EX / BR	EM / EX / BR	EM / EX / BR	EM / EX / BR	EM / EX / BR
_____	EM / EX / BR	EM / EX / BR	EM / EX / BR	EM / EX / BR	EM / EX / BR
_____	EM / EX / BR	EM / EX / BR	EM / EX / BR	EM / EX / BR	EM / EX / BR
_____	EM / EX / BR	EM / EX / BR	EM / EX / BR	EM / EX / BR	EM / EX / BR
_____	EM / EX / BR	EM / EX / BR	EM / EX / BR	EM / EX / BR	EM / EX / BR
_____	EM / EX / BR	EM / EX / BR	EM / EX / BR	EM / EX / BR	EM / EX / BR
_____	EM / EX / BR	EM / EX / BR	EM / EX / BR	EM / EX / BR	EM / EX / BR
_____	EM / EX / BR	EM / EX / BR	EM / EX / BR	EM / EX / BR	EM / EX / BR
_____	EM / EX / BR	EM / EX / BR	EM / EX / BR	EM / EX / BR	EM / EX / BR
_____	EM / EX / BR	EM / EX / BR	EM / EX / BR	EM / EX / BR	EM / EX / BR
_____	EM / EX / BR	EM / EX / BR	EM / EX / BR	EM / EX / BR	EM / EX / BR
_____	EM / EX / BR	EM / EX / BR	EM / EX / BR	EM / EX / BR	EM / EX / BR
_____	EM / EX / BR	EM / EX / BR	EM / EX / BR	EM / EX / BR	EM / EX / BR
_____	EM / EX / BR	EM / EX / BR	EM / EX / BR	EM / EX / BR	EM / EX / BR
_____	EM / EX / BR	EM / EX / BR	EM / EX / BR	EM / EX / BR	EM / EX / BR

Writing: *Write About Academic Information*

ELD Standards Record Sheet

Teacher: _____ **Class:** _____

Standards: *PII.B.3*   **Guided Activities and Proficiency Levels:**

Students:	#1	#2	#3	#4	#5
	EM / EX / BR	EM / EX / BR	EM / EX / BR	EM / EX / BR	EM / EX / BR
	EM / EX / BR	EM / EX / BR	EM / EX / BR	EM / EX / BR	EM / EX / BR
	EM / EX / BR	EM / EX / BR	EM / EX / BR	EM / EX / BR	EM / EX / BR
	EM / EX / BR	EM / EX / BR	EM / EX / BR	EM / EX / BR	EM / EX / BR
	EM / EX / BR	EM / EX / BR	EM / EX / BR	EM / EX / BR	EM / EX / BR
	EM / EX / BR	EM / EX / BR	EM / EX / BR	EM / EX / BR	EM / EX / BR
	EM / EX / BR	EM / EX / BR	EM / EX / BR	EM / EX / BR	EM / EX / BR
	EM / EX / BR	EM / EX / BR	EM / EX / BR	EM / EX / BR	EM / EX / BR
	EM / EX / BR	EM / EX / BR	EM / EX / BR	EM / EX / BR	EM / EX / BR
	EM / EX / BR	EM / EX / BR	EM / EX / BR	EM / EX / BR	EM / EX / BR
	EM / EX / BR	EM / EX / BR	EM / EX / BR	EM / EX / BR	EM / EX / BR
	EM / EX / BR	EM / EX / BR	EM / EX / BR	EM / EX / BR	EM / EX / BR
	EM / EX / BR	EM / EX / BR	EM / EX / BR	EM / EX / BR	EM / EX / BR
	EM / EX / BR	EM / EX / BR	EM / EX / BR	EM / EX / BR	EM / EX / BR
	EM / EX / BR	EM / EX / BR	EM / EX / BR	EM / EX / BR	EM / EX / BR
	EM / EX / BR	EM / EX / BR	EM / EX / BR	EM / EX / BR	EM / EX / BR
	EM / EX / BR	EM / EX / BR	EM / EX / BR	EM / EX / BR	EM / EX / BR
	EM / EX / BR	EM / EX / BR	EM / EX / BR	EM / EX / BR	EM / EX / BR
	EM / EX / BR	EM / EX / BR	EM / EX / BR	EM / EX / BR	EM / EX / BR
	EM / EX / BR	EM / EX / BR	EM / EX / BR	EM / EX / BR	EM / EX / BR

Writing: *Write About Academic Information*

ELD Standards Record Sheet

Teacher: _____ **Class:** _____

Standards: *PII.B.4*   **Guided Activities and Proficiency Levels:**

Students:	#1	#2	#3	#4	#5
_____	EM / EX / BR	EM / EX / BR	EM / EX / BR	EM / EX / BR	EM / EX / BR
_____	EM / EX / BR	EM / EX / BR	EM / EX / BR	EM / EX / BR	EM / EX / BR
_____	EM / EX / BR	EM / EX / BR	EM / EX / BR	EM / EX / BR	EM / EX / BR
_____	EM / EX / BR	EM / EX / BR	EM / EX / BR	EM / EX / BR	EM / EX / BR
_____	EM / EX / BR	EM / EX / BR	EM / EX / BR	EM / EX / BR	EM / EX / BR
_____	EM / EX / BR	EM / EX / BR	EM / EX / BR	EM / EX / BR	EM / EX / BR
_____	EM / EX / BR	EM / EX / BR	EM / EX / BR	EM / EX / BR	EM / EX / BR
_____	EM / EX / BR	EM / EX / BR	EM / EX / BR	EM / EX / BR	EM / EX / BR
_____	EM / EX / BR	EM / EX / BR	EM / EX / BR	EM / EX / BR	EM / EX / BR
_____	EM / EX / BR	EM / EX / BR	EM / EX / BR	EM / EX / BR	EM / EX / BR
_____	EM / EX / BR	EM / EX / BR	EM / EX / BR	EM / EX / BR	EM / EX / BR
_____	EM / EX / BR	EM / EX / BR	EM / EX / BR	EM / EX / BR	EM / EX / BR
_____	EM / EX / BR	EM / EX / BR	EM / EX / BR	EM / EX / BR	EM / EX / BR
_____	EM / EX / BR	EM / EX / BR	EM / EX / BR	EM / EX / BR	EM / EX / BR
_____	EM / EX / BR	EM / EX / BR	EM / EX / BR	EM / EX / BR	EM / EX / BR
_____	EM / EX / BR	EM / EX / BR	EM / EX / BR	EM / EX / BR	EM / EX / BR
_____	EM / EX / BR	EM / EX / BR	EM / EX / BR	EM / EX / BR	EM / EX / BR
_____	EM / EX / BR	EM / EX / BR	EM / EX / BR	EM / EX / BR	EM / EX / BR
_____	EM / EX / BR	EM / EX / BR	EM / EX / BR	EM / EX / BR	EM / EX / BR
_____	EM / EX / BR	EM / EX / BR	EM / EX / BR	EM / EX / BR	EM / EX / BR

Writing: *Write About Academic Information*

ELD Standards Record Sheet

Teacher: _____ **Class:** _____

Standards: *PII.B.5* **Guided Activities and Proficiency Levels:**

Students:	#1	#2	#3	#4	#5
_____	EM / EX / BR	EM / EX / BR	EM / EX / BR	EM / EX / BR	EM / EX / BR
_____	EM / EX / BR	EM / EX / BR	EM / EX / BR	EM / EX / BR	EM / EX / BR
_____	EM / EX / BR	EM / EX / BR	EM / EX / BR	EM / EX / BR	EM / EX / BR
_____	EM / EX / BR	EM / EX / BR	EM / EX / BR	EM / EX / BR	EM / EX / BR
_____	EM / EX / BR	EM / EX / BR	EM / EX / BR	EM / EX / BR	EM / EX / BR
_____	EM / EX / BR	EM / EX / BR	EM / EX / BR	EM / EX / BR	EM / EX / BR
_____	EM / EX / BR	EM / EX / BR	EM / EX / BR	EM / EX / BR	EM / EX / BR
_____	EM / EX / BR	EM / EX / BR	EM / EX / BR	EM / EX / BR	EM / EX / BR
_____	EM / EX / BR	EM / EX / BR	EM / EX / BR	EM / EX / BR	EM / EX / BR
_____	EM / EX / BR	EM / EX / BR	EM / EX / BR	EM / EX / BR	EM / EX / BR
_____	EM / EX / BR	EM / EX / BR	EM / EX / BR	EM / EX / BR	EM / EX / BR
_____	EM / EX / BR	EM / EX / BR	EM / EX / BR	EM / EX / BR	EM / EX / BR
_____	EM / EX / BR	EM / EX / BR	EM / EX / BR	EM / EX / BR	EM / EX / BR
_____	EM / EX / BR	EM / EX / BR	EM / EX / BR	EM / EX / BR	EM / EX / BR
_____	EM / EX / BR	EM / EX / BR	EM / EX / BR	EM / EX / BR	EM / EX / BR
_____	EM / EX / BR	EM / EX / BR	EM / EX / BR	EM / EX / BR	EM / EX / BR
_____	EM / EX / BR	EM / EX / BR	EM / EX / BR	EM / EX / BR	EM / EX / BR
_____	EM / EX / BR	EM / EX / BR	EM / EX / BR	EM / EX / BR	EM / EX / BR
_____	EM / EX / BR	EM / EX / BR	EM / EX / BR	EM / EX / BR	EM / EX / BR
_____	EM / EX / BR	EM / EX / BR	EM / EX / BR	EM / EX / BR	EM / EX / BR

ELD Standards Record Sheet

Teacher: _____ **Class:** _____

Standards: *PII.C.6*   **Guided Activities and Proficiency Levels:**

Students:	#1	#2	#3	#4	#5
	EM / EX / BR	EM / EX / BR	EM / EX / BR	EM / EX / BR	EM / EX / BR
	EM / EX / BR	EM / EX / BR	EM / EX / BR	EM / EX / BR	EM / EX / BR
	EM / EX / BR	EM / EX / BR	EM / EX / BR	EM / EX / BR	EM / EX / BR
	EM / EX / BR	EM / EX / BR	EM / EX / BR	EM / EX / BR	EM / EX / BR
	EM / EX / BR	EM / EX / BR	EM / EX / BR	EM / EX / BR	EM / EX / BR
	EM / EX / BR	EM / EX / BR	EM / EX / BR	EM / EX / BR	EM / EX / BR
	EM / EX / BR	EM / EX / BR	EM / EX / BR	EM / EX / BR	EM / EX / BR
	EM / EX / BR	EM / EX / BR	EM / EX / BR	EM / EX / BR	EM / EX / BR
	EM / EX / BR	EM / EX / BR	EM / EX / BR	EM / EX / BR	EM / EX / BR
	EM / EX / BR	EM / EX / BR	EM / EX / BR	EM / EX / BR	EM / EX / BR
	EM / EX / BR	EM / EX / BR	EM / EX / BR	EM / EX / BR	EM / EX / BR
	EM / EX / BR	EM / EX / BR	EM / EX / BR	EM / EX / BR	EM / EX / BR
	EM / EX / BR	EM / EX / BR	EM / EX / BR	EM / EX / BR	EM / EX / BR
	EM / EX / BR	EM / EX / BR	EM / EX / BR	EM / EX / BR	EM / EX / BR
	EM / EX / BR	EM / EX / BR	EM / EX / BR	EM / EX / BR	EM / EX / BR
	EM / EX / BR	EM / EX / BR	EM / EX / BR	EM / EX / BR	EM / EX / BR
	EM / EX / BR	EM / EX / BR	EM / EX / BR	EM / EX / BR	EM / EX / BR
	EM / EX / BR	EM / EX / BR	EM / EX / BR	EM / EX / BR	EM / EX / BR
	EM / EX / BR	EM / EX / BR	EM / EX / BR	EM / EX / BR	EM / EX / BR

Writing: *Write About Academic Information*

ELD Standards Record Sheet

Teacher: _____ **Class:** _____

Standards: *PII.C.7*

Guided Activities and Proficiency Levels:

Students:	#1	#2	#3	#4	#5
	EM / EX / BR	EM / EX / BR	EM / EX / BR	EM / EX / BR	EM / EX / BR
	EM / EX / BR	EM / EX / BR	EM / EX / BR	EM / EX / BR	EM / EX / BR
	EM / EX / BR	EM / EX / BR	EM / EX / BR	EM / EX / BR	EM / EX / BR
	EM / EX / BR	EM / EX / BR	EM / EX / BR	EM / EX / BR	EM / EX / BR
	EM / EX / BR	EM / EX / BR	EM / EX / BR	EM / EX / BR	EM / EX / BR
	EM / EX / BR	EM / EX / BR	EM / EX / BR	EM / EX / BR	EM / EX / BR
	EM / EX / BR	EM / EX / BR	EM / EX / BR	EM / EX / BR	EM / EX / BR
	EM / EX / BR	EM / EX / BR	EM / EX / BR	EM / EX / BR	EM / EX / BR
	EM / EX / BR	EM / EX / BR	EM / EX / BR	EM / EX / BR	EM / EX / BR
	EM / EX / BR	EM / EX / BR	EM / EX / BR	EM / EX / BR	EM / EX / BR
	EM / EX / BR	EM / EX / BR	EM / EX / BR	EM / EX / BR	EM / EX / BR
	EM / EX / BR	EM / EX / BR	EM / EX / BR	EM / EX / BR	EM / EX / BR
	EM / EX / BR	EM / EX / BR	EM / EX / BR	EM / EX / BR	EM / EX / BR
	EM / EX / BR	EM / EX / BR	EM / EX / BR	EM / EX / BR	EM / EX / BR
	EM / EX / BR	EM / EX / BR	EM / EX / BR	EM / EX / BR	EM / EX / BR
	EM / EX / BR	EM / EX / BR	EM / EX / BR	EM / EX / BR	EM / EX / BR
	EM / EX / BR	EM / EX / BR	EM / EX / BR	EM / EX / BR	EM / EX / BR
	EM / EX / BR	EM / EX / BR	EM / EX / BR	EM / EX / BR	EM / EX / BR
	EM / EX / BR	EM / EX / BR	EM / EX / BR	EM / EX / BR	EM / EX / BR
	EM / EX / BR	EM / EX / BR	EM / EX / BR	EM / EX / BR	EM / EX / BR

Writing Activity #1

Name: _____

Directions: Look at the academic details in the graphic organizer. Use the sentence starters and details to help you write a complete sentence for each section.

Animal

American Bullfrog
(amphibian)

The .... is an ....
           (animal name)   *(type)*

Appearance
- small, 6 to 8 inches
- brown or green in color
- dark spots on back
- webbed feet

It is ...
_____
_____

Habitat
- freshwater, ponds, lakes, marshes
- warm weather
- mainly found in the eastern and central parts of North America

These animals live in ...
_____
_____

Diet
- insects
- mice
- snakes
- fish

Its diet consists of ...
_____
_____

Predators
- turtles
- snakes
- birds
- humans

One type of predator that hunts this animal is ....
_____
_____

Writing Activity #1 - cont'd

Name: _____

Directions: Rewrite and organize the sentences you wrote into paragraph form. <u>You can add more sentences, if you choose.</u> Write your paragraph in the box below.

Writing Activity #2

Name: ....

Directions: Look at the academic details in the graphic organizer. Use the sentence
starters and details to help you write a complete sentence for each section.

Country **Japan** *(capital: Tokyo)*	*(name of country)* *The country is* .... *and the capital is* .... *(capital)*

Location
- off the coast of eastern Asia
- in western Pacific Ocean
- group of islands
- biggest island is Honshu

It is located ...

_____

_____

Government
- over 126.5 million people
- parliamentary system with a prime minister
- constitutional monarchy with an emperor

The government is ...

_____

_____

Food
- sushi and seafood
- noodles like udon and ramen
- rice
- miso soup and vegetables

Different types of food are ...

_____

_____

Culture
- religion is Shinto and Buddhism
- many temples everywhere
- deeply rooted in traditions
- advanced technology

The culture ....

_____

_____

Writing Activity #2 - cont'd

Name:

Directions: Rewrite and organize the sentences you wrote into paragraph form. <u>You can add more sentences, if you choose.</u> Write your paragraph in the box below.

Writing Activity #3

Name: _____

Directions: Look at the academic details in the graphic organizer. Use the sentence starters and details to help you write a complete sentence for each section.

Energy

Renewable Energy
(natural resources)

.... *comes from* ....
(type of energy)   (what resources)

Types
- wind power (wind)
- hydropower (water)
- solar power (sun)
- biofuel (organic waste)

One type of renewable energy is …
_____
_____

Benefits
- abundant and unlimited
- comes from the environment
- reduces air pollution
- creates more jobs (good for economy)

A benefit to renewable energy is …
_____
_____

Challenges
- can be very expensive
- dependent on the environment and weather
- requires a lot of energy

One challenge to renewable energy is …
_____
_____

Nonrenewable Energy
- nuclear energy
- oil
- natural gas
- coal

An example of nonrenewable energy is ….
_____
_____

Writing Activity #3 - cont'd

Name:

Directions: Rewrite and organize the sentences you wrote into paragraph form. <u>You can add more sentences, if you choose.</u> Write your paragraph in the box below.

Writing Activity #4

Name: _____

Directions: Look at the academic details in the graphic organizer. Use the sentence starters and details to help you write a complete sentence for each section.

Animal

Bald Eagle
(bird)

The .... is a ....
(animal name)   (type)

Appearance
- white head and neck (that's why it's called bald)
- large wingspan (over 7.5 feet)
- brown body

One thing about its appearance is ...
_____
_____

Habitat
- mainly lives in North America (US, Canada, and Mexico)
- build nests in tall trees
- lives near water (sea, rivers, lakes)

Its habitat is ...
_____
_____

Diet
- fish (trout, salmon)
- scavengers of dead animals
- small animals (mice, rabbits, frogs, etc.)

Its diet includes ...
_____
_____

Interesting facts
- really good eyesight (can see a fish up to 1 mile away)
- they can hunt and catch with just their talons/claws

One interesting fact is ....
_____
_____

Writing Activity #4 - cont'd

Name:

Directions: Rewrite and organize the sentences you wrote into paragraph form. <u>You can add more sentences, if you choose.</u> Write your paragraph in the box below.

Writing Activity #5

Name: _____

Directions: Look at the academic details in the graphic organizer. Use the sentence starters and details to help you write a complete sentence for each section.

Biome

Deserts
(driest)

The .... are the .... biomes.
   (name of biome)   *(description)*

Location
- Sahara (largest desert) is in Africa
- North Africa
- Western Americas
- Central Australia

These large areas of ecosystems are located ...
_____
_____

Climate
- very little rainfall (less than 10 inches per year)
- temperatures: daytime as high as 120°F, night time as low as 32°F
- sandstorms

The climate, or weather, is ...
_____
_____

Animals
- survives with very little water
- lizards and snakes
- small rodents
- camels

Animals living in these biomes ...
_____
_____

Plants
- stores water in its stems
- shallow roots to absorb rainfall
- cactus
- small bushes

Plants living in these biomes ....
_____
_____

Writing Activity #5 - cont'd

Name:

Directions: Rewrite and organize the sentences you wrote into paragraph form. <u>You can add more sentences, if you choose.</u> Write your paragraph in the box below.

Writing Activity - *Blank Template*

Name: _____

Directions: Look at the academic details in the graphic organizer. Use the sentence starters and details to help you write a complete sentence for each section.

Writing Activity - *Blank Template*

Name: _____

Directions: Rewrite and organize the sentences you wrote into paragraph form. <u>You can add more sentences, if you choose.</u> Write your paragraph in the box below.

_____
_____
_____
_____
_____
_____
_____
_____
_____
_____
_____
_____
_____
_____
_____
_____
_____
_____
_____
_____
_____

Writing
Justify an Opinion

This section includes:
- Guided Activities
- Teacher's ELD Standards Record Sheet
- Student Practice Activities:
  - Graphic organizers
  - Opinion writing practice
  - Bonus blank writing template

- -

Alignment to CA ELD Standards:

Part I: Interacting in Meaningful Ways
<u>C.11 Supporting Opinions</u>
Supporting own opinions and evaluating others' opinions in speaking and writing

Alignment to CCSS:

W.3.1, 4, 10; SL.3.4, 6; L.3.1–3, 6
W.4.1, 4, 9–10; SL.4.4, 6; L.4.1–3, 6
W.5.1, 4, 9–10; SL.5.4, 6; L.5.1–3, 6

Part I: Interacting in Meaningful Ways
<u>C.12 Selecting Language Resources</u>
Selecting and applying varied and precise vocabulary and language structures to effectively convey ideas

W.3.4–5; SL.3.4, 6; L.3.1, 3, 5–6
W.4.4–5; SL.4.4, 6; L.4.1, 3, 5–6
W.5.4–5; SL.5.4, 6; L.5.1, 3, 5–6

Part II: Learning About How English Works
<u>A.1 Structuring Cohesive Texts</u>
Understanding text structure

RL.3.5; RI.3.5; W.3.1–5; SL.3.4
RL.4.5; RI.4.5; W.4.1–5; SL.4.4
RL.5.5; RI.5.5; W.5.1–5; SL.5.4

Part II: Learning About How English Works
<u>B.3 Expanding and Enriching Ideas</u>
Using verbs and verb phrases

W.3.5; SL.3.6; L.3.1, 3, 6
W.4.5; SL.4.6; L.4.1, 3, 6
W.5.5; SL.5.6; L.5.1, 3, 6

Part II: Learning About How English Works
<u>B.4 Expanding and Enriching Ideas</u>
Using nouns and noun phrases

W.3.5; SL.3.6; L.3.1, 3, 6
W.4.5; SL.4.6; L.4.1, 3, 6
W.5.5; SL.5.6; L.5.1, 3, 6

Part II: Learning About How English Works
<u>B.5 Expanding and Enriching Ideas</u>
Modifying to add details

W.3.5; SL.3.4, 6; L.3.1, 3, 6
W.4.5; SL.4.4, 6; L.4.1, 3, 6
W.5.5; SL.5.4, 6; L.5.1, 3, 6

Part II: Learning About How English Works
<u>C.6 Connecting and Condensing Ideas</u>
Connecting ideas

W.3.1-3, 5; SL.3.4, 6; L.3.1, 3, 6
W.4.1–3, 5; SL.4.4, 6; L.4.1, 3, 6
W.5.1–3, 5; SL.5.4, 6; L.5.1, 3, 6

- -

Writing
Justify an Opinion

Guided Activities Direction:

1. Show students the writing prompt
2. Explain to the students that they'll be writing an essay about a school-related issue as if they will be giving it to the principal
3. Guide students through:
   - Reading the directions and prompt carefully
   - Understanding what should be included in their writing
   - Understanding if revisions to their writing is necessary
4. Then have students practice with additional writing activities for justifying an opinion

....

Guiding Descriptors
Use the following guidelines to assist students with their writing.

- Guide students in explicitly expressing their opinion or stating their position on the issue

- Guide students in supporting their opinions with at least **TWO** relevant and detailed reasons

- Guide students in using well-developed descriptions, details, and/or examples

- Help students make sure that their response is readily coherent

- Help students with their grammar and word choice

- Help students with their spelling and punctuation

- Guide students in writing a response that includes a paragraph of at least **THREE or more** sentences

Guided Activity #1

Name: _____

Directions: You are going to write at least <u>one paragraph</u> in English about an important issue.

- Think about what you will write before you begin writing.
- State your opinion clearly and give two or more reasons to support your opinion.
- The paragraph should include at least three complete sentences.
- Check your writing for correct grammar, capital letters, punctuation, and spelling.
- Do now write outside the box. Please write neatly.

Writing Prompt: *The cafeteria manager in your school has decided to put in a soda vending machine. Do you think that it is a good idea that students can buy soda at school?* Write at least one paragraph in support of your opinion to give to your principal. Make sure you write at least three sentences and include your opinion and supporting reasons.

Guided Activity #2

Name:

Directions: You are going to write at least <u>one paragraph</u> in English about an important issue.

- Think about what you will write before you begin writing.
- State your opinion clearly and give two or more reasons to support your opinion.
- The paragraph should include at least three complete sentences.
- Check your writing for correct grammar, capital letters, punctuation, and spelling.
- Do now write outside the box. Please write neatly.

<u>Writing Prompt:</u> *The teachers in your school have decided to eliminate all tests for the rest of the year. Do you think that it is a good idea for teachers to not give any tests to students?* Write at least one paragraph in support of your opinion to give to your principal. Make sure you write at least three sentences and include your opinion and supporting reasons.

Guided Activity #3

Name: _____

Directions: You are going to write at least <u>one paragraph</u> in English about an important issue.

- Think about what you will write before you begin writing.
- State your opinion clearly and give two or more reasons to support your opinion.
- The paragraph should include at least three complete sentences.
- Check your writing for correct grammar, capital letters, punctuation, and spelling.
- Do now write outside the box. Please write neatly.

<u>**Writing Prompt:**</u> **The student council in your school has voted to eliminate all sports from being played at school. Do you think that it is a good idea for sports to be taken away at school?** Write at least one paragraph in support of your opinion to give to your principal. Make sure you write at least three sentences and include your opinion and supporting reasons.

Writing: *Justify an Opinion*

Guided Activity #4

Name:

Directions: You are going to write at least <u>one paragraph</u> in English about an important issue.

- Think about what you will write before you begin writing.
- State your opinion clearly and give two or more reasons to support your opinion.
- The paragraph should include at least three complete sentences.
- Check your writing for correct grammar, capital letters, punctuation, and spelling.
- Do now write outside the box. Please write neatly.

Writing Prompt: *The parent school board in your school has decided to make student uniforms mandatory. Do you think that it is a good idea for students to wear school uniforms?* Write at least one paragraph in support of your opinion to give to your principal. Make sure you write at least three sentences and include your opinion and supporting reasons.

Guided Activity #5

Name: _____

Directions: You are going to write at least <u>one paragraph</u> in English about an important issue.

- Think about what you will write before you begin writing.
- State your opinion clearly and give two or more reasons to support your opinion.
- The paragraph should include at least three complete sentences.
- Check your writing for correct grammar, capital letters, punctuation, and spelling.
- Do now write outside the box. Please write neatly.

<u>Writing Prompt:</u> *The teachers in your school have decided to give an extra hour of homework everyday. Do you think that it is a good idea for teachers to give extra homework?* Write at least one paragraph in support of your opinion to give to your principal. Make sure you write at least three sentences and include your opinion and supporting reasons.

ELD Standards Record Sheet

Directions:

1. Look at the CA ELD standards (**BELOW**) that correspond to this section.
2. Reference these specific standards for the template Record Sheet.
3. Use the following template Record Sheet to monitor students' proficiency levels for the **GUIDED ACTIVITIES** in this section.
4. Fill out all the information. Circle, check, highlight the proficiency level. (*There is space for 20 students. Make additional copies, as needed*)
5. Retain for your records to be used during grading, parent/student conferences, lesson planning, ELD documentation, etc.

Suggestion: You can make one copy of each guided activity and/or the student practice sheets and laminate them. Organize the laminated sheets onto a book ring. Now it'll be easily accessible for whole group, small group, one-on-one, centers, etc. Copy as many of the ELD Standards Record Sheet as you need and keep it handy along with the activities.

ELD Standards Record Sheet

CA ELD Standards & Proficiency Levels
Part I: Interacting in Meaningful Ways
C.11 Supporting Opinions

EMERGING (EM) ⟶	EXPANDING (EX) ⟶	BRIDGING (BR)
Requires **Substantial** Support	Requires **Moderate** Support	Requires **Light** Support
GRADE 3		

• Support opinions by providing:
  ○ good reasons
  ○ some textual evidence
  ○ relevant background knowledge (e.g. referring to textual evidence or knowledge of content)
	• Support opinions by providing:
	  ○ good reasons
	  ○ <u>increasingly detailed</u> textual evidence
	  ○ relevant background knowledge <u>about the content</u> (e.g. providing examples from the text)
		• Support opinions or <u>persuade others</u> by providing:
		  ○ good reasons
		  ○ <u>detailed</u> textual evidence
		  ○ relevant background knowledge about the content (e.g. specific evidence or graphics from text)

GRADE 4		

• Support opinions by expressing appropriate/accurate reasons using:
  ○ textual evidence (e.g. referring to text)
  ○ relevant background knowledge about content
• Requires substantial support
• Express ideas and opinions or expressions (e.g. can, will, maybe)
	• Support opinions or <u>persuade others</u> by expressing appropriate/accurate reasons using:
	  ○ <u>Some</u> textual evidence (e.g. Paraphrasing facts)
	  ○ relevant background knowledge about content
	  ○ Requires <u>moderate</u> support
	  ○ Express <u>attitude</u> and opinions or <u>temper statements with familiar modal</u> expressions (e.g. maybe/probably, can/must)
		• Support opinions or persuade others by expressing appropriate/accurate reasons using:
		  ○ <u>Detailed</u> textual evidence (e.g. Quotations or specific events from text)
		  ○ relevant background knowledge about content
		• Requires <u>light</u> support
		• Express attitude and opinions or temper statements with <u>nuanced modal</u> expressions (e.g. probably/certainly, should/would) and paraphrasing (e.g. In my opinion...)

GRADE 5		

• Support opinions by expressing appropriate/accurate reasons using:
  ○ textual evidence (e.g. referring to text)
  ○ relevant background knowledge about content
• Requires substantial support
• Express ideas and opinions or expressions (e.g. can, will, maybe)
	• Support opinions or <u>persuade others</u> by expressing appropriate/accurate reasons using:
	  ○ <u>Some</u> textual evidence (e.g. paraphrasing facts)
	  ○ relevant background knowledge about content
	• Requires <u>moderate</u> support
	• Express <u>attitude</u> and opinions or <u>temper statements with familiar modal</u> expressions (e.g. maybe/probably, can/must)
		• Support opinions or persuade others by expressing appropriate/accurate reasons using:
		  ○ <u>Detailed</u> textual evidence (e.g. Quotations or specific events from text)
		  ○ relevant background knowledge about content
		• Requires <u>light</u> support
		• Express attitude and opinions or temper statements with <u>nuanced modal</u> expressions (e.g. probably/certainly, should/would) and paraphrasing (e.g. In my opinion...)

ELD Standards Record Sheet

CA ELD Standards & Proficiency Levels
Part I: Interacting in Meaningful Ways
C.12 Selecting Language Resources

EMERGING (EM)	EXPANDING (EX)	BRIDGING (BR)
Requires **Substantial** Support	Requires **Moderate** Support	Requires **Light** Support
GRADE 3		
• Use a select number of general academic and domain-specific words: ○ to add detail (e.g. adding the word dangerous to describe a place, using the word habitat when describing animal behavior) • Uses the words while speaking and writing	• Use a growing number of general academic and domain-specific words in order to: ○ add detail ○ create an effect (e.g. using the word suddenly to signal a change) ○ create shades of meaning (e.g.scurry vs. dash) • Uses the words while speaking and writing	• Use a wide variety of general academic and domain-specific words , synonyms, antonyms, and non-literal language to: ○ create an effect ○ precision ○ shades of meaning • Uses the words while speaking and writing
GRADE 4		
• Use a select number of general academic and domain-specific words to create precision while speaking and writing • Select a few frequently used affixes for accuracy and precision (e.g. She walks, I'm unhappy.)	• Use a growing number of general academic and domain-specific words, synonyms, and antonyms to create precision and shades of meaning while speaking and writing • Select a growing number of frequently used affixes for accuracy and precision (e.g. She walked. He likes…, I'm unhappy.)	• Use a wide variety number of general academic and domain-specific words, synonyms, and antonyms, and figurative language to create precision and shades of meaning while speaking and writing • Select a variety of appropriate affixes for accuracy and precision (e.g. She walking. I'm uncomfortable. They left reluctantly.)
GRADE 5		
• Use a select number of general academic and domain-specific words to create precision while speaking and writing • Select a few frequently used affixes for accuracy and precision (e.g. She walks, I'm unhappy.)	• Use a growing number of general academic and domain-specific words, synonyms, and antonyms to create precision and shades of meaning while speaking and writing • Select a growing number of frequently used affixes for accuracy and precision (e.g. She walked. He likes…, I'm unhappy.)	• Use a wide variety number of general academic and domain-specific words, synonyms, and antonyms, and figurative language to create precision and shades of meaning while speaking and writing • Select a variety of appropriate affixes for accuracy and precision (e.g. She walking. I'm uncomfortable. They left reluctantly.)

Writing: *Justify an Opinion*

ELD Standards Record Sheet

CA ELD Standards & Proficiency Levels:
Part II: Learning About How English Works
A.1 Understanding Text Structure

EMERGING (EM)	EXPANDING (EX)	BRIDGING (BR)
Requires **Substantial** Support	Requires **Moderate** Support	Requires **Light** Support
GRADE 3		
• Apply understanding of how text types are organized to express ideas (e.g. how a story is organized sequentially) • Comprehend & compose basic texts	• Apply understanding of how different text types are organized to express ideas (e.g. how a story is organized sequentially with predictable stages) • Comprehend & write texts (<u>w/ increasing cohesion</u>)	• Apply understanding of how different text types are organized to express ideas (e.g. how a story is organized sequentially with predictable stages versus how opinion/arguments are structured logically, grouping related ideas) • Comprehend & write <u>cohesive</u> texts
GRADE 4		
• Apply understanding of how different text types are organized to express ideas (e.g. how a narrative is organized sequentially) • Comprehend & compose basic texts	• Apply <u>increasing</u> understanding of how different text types are organized to express ideas (e.g. how a narrative is organized sequentially with predictable stages vs how an explanation is organized around ideas) • Comprehend & write texts (<u>w/ increasing cohesion</u>)	• Apply understanding of how different text types are organized to express ideas (e.g. how a narrative is organized sequentially with predictable stages versus how opinion/arguments are structured logically, grouping related ideas) • Comprehend & write <u>cohesive</u> texts
GRADE 5		
• Apply basic understanding of how different text types are organized to express ideas (e.g. how a narrative is organized sequentially with predictable stages vs how opinions/ arguments are organized around ideas) • Comprehend & compose basic texts	• Apply <u>growing</u> understanding of how different text types are organized to express ideas (e.g. how a narrative is organized sequentially with predictable stages vs how opinions/ arguments are structured logically around reasons and evidence) • Comprehend & write texts (<u>w/ increasing cohesion</u>)	• Apply <u>increasing</u> understanding of how different text types are organized to express ideas (e.g. how a historical account is organized chronologically vs how opinions/arguments are structured logically around reasons and evidence) • Comprehend & write <u>cohesive</u> texts

ELD Standards Record Sheet

CA ELD Standards & Proficiency Levels

Part II: Learning About How English Works
B.3 Using Verbs and Verb Phrases

EMERGING (EM)	EXPANDING (EX)	BRIDGING (BR)
Requires **Substantial** Support	Requires **Moderate** Support	Requires **Light** Support
GRADE 3		
• Use frequently used verbs • Use different verb types (e.g. doing, saying, being/having, thinking/feeling) • Use different verb tenses (e.g. simple past for recounting an experience) • Appropriate for the text type and discipline to convey time	• Use a growing number of verb types (e.g. doing, saying, being/having, thinking/feeling) • Use a growing number of verb tenses (e.g. simple past for retelling, simple present for a science description) • Appropriate for the text type and discipline to convey time	• Use a variety of verb types (e.g. doing, saying, being/having, thinking/feeling) • Use a variety of verb tenses (e.g. simple present for a science description, simple future to predict) • Appropriate for the text type and discipline to convey time
GRADE 4		
• Use various verbs • Use various verb types (e.g. doing, saying, being/having, thinking/feeling) • Use various verb tenses (e.g. simple past for recounting an experience) • Appropriate for the text type and discipline for familiar topics	• Use various verbs • Use various verb types (e.g. doing, saying, being/having, thinking/feeling) • Use various verb tenses (e.g. simple past for retelling, timeless present for science explanation) • Appropriate for the task, text type and discipline • For an increasing variety of familiar and new topics	• Use various verb • Use various verb types (e.g. doing, saying, being/having, thinking/feeling) • Use various verb tenses(e.g. timeless present for science explanation, mixture of past and present for historical information report) • Appropriate for the task and text type • For a variety of familiar and new topics
GRADE 5		
• Use frequently used verbs (e.g. take, like, eat) • Use various verb types (e.g. doing, saying, being/having, thinking/feeling) • Use various verb tenses (e.g. simple past for recounting an experience) • Appropriate for the text type and discipline for familiar topics	• Use various verb types (e.g. doing, saying, being/having, thinking/feeling) • Use various verb tenses (e.g. simple past for retelling, timeless present for science a description) • Appropriate for the task, text type and discipline • For an increasing variety of topics	• Use various verb types (e.g. doing, saying, being/having, thinking/feeling) • Use various verb tenses (e.g. timeless present for science description, mixture of past and present for narrative or history explanation) • Appropriate for the task and text type • For a variety of topics

Writing: *Justify an Opinion*

ELD Standards Record Sheet

CA ELD Standards & Proficiency Levels

Part II: Learning About How English Works
B.4 Using Nouns and Noun Phrases

EMERGING (EM)	EXPANDING (EX)	BRIDGING (BR)
Requires **Substantial** Support	Requires **Moderate** Support	Requires **Light** Support
GRADE 3		

• Expand noun phrases in simple ways in order to enrich:
  ○ The meaning of sentences
  ○ Add details about ideas, people, things, etc. (e.g. adding an adjective to a noun)
	• Expand noun phrases in a <u>growing number</u> of ways in order to enrich:
	  ○ The meaning of sentences
	  ○ Add details about ideas, people, things, etc. (e.g. adding comparative/superlative adjectives to nouns)
		• Expand noun phrases in a <u>variety</u> of ways in order to enrich:
		  ○ The meaning of sentences and
		  ○ Add details about ideas, people, things, etc. (e.g. adding comparative/superlative adjectives to nouns, simple clause embedding)

GRADE 4		

• Expand noun phrases in simple ways in order to enrich:
  ○ The meaning of sentences
  ○ Add details about ideas, people, things, etc. (e.g. adding an adjective)
	• Expand noun phrases in a <u>variety</u> of ways in order to enrich:
	  ○ The meaning of sentences
	  ○ Add details about ideas, people, things, etc. (e.g. adding adjectives to noun phrases or simple clause embedding)
		• Expand noun phrases in an <u>increasing variety</u> of ways in order to enrich:
		  ○ The meaning of sentences and
		  ○ Add details about ideas, people, things, etc. (e.g. adding general academic adjectives and adverbs to noun phrases or more complex clause embedding)

GRADE 5		

• Expand noun phrases in simple ways in order to enrich:
  ○ The meaning of sentences
  ○ Add details about ideas, people, things, etc. (e.g. adding an adjective to a noun)
	• Expand noun phrases in a <u>variety</u> of ways in order to enrich:
	  ○ The meaning of sentences
	  ○ Add details about ideas, people, things, etc. (e.g. adding comparative/superlative adjectives to noun phrases or simple clause embedding)
		• Expand noun phrases in an <u>increasing variety</u> of ways in order to enrich:
		  ○ The meaning of sentences
		  ○ Add details about ideas, people, things, etc. (e.g. adding comparative/superlative and general academic adjectives to noun phrases or more complex clause embedding)

ELD Standards Record Sheet

CA ELD Standards & Proficiency Levels

Part II: Learning About How English Works
B.5 Modifying to Add Details

EMERGING (EM)	EXPANDING (EX)	BRIDGING (BR)
Requires **Substantial** Support	Requires **Moderate** Support	Requires **Light** Support
GRADE 3		
• Expand sentences with adverbials (e.g. adverbs, adverb phrases, prepositional phrases) • Use these to provide details about a familiar activity or process (e.g. time, manner, place, cause) (e.g. They walked to the soccer field.)	• Expand sentences with adverbials (e.g. adverbs, adverb phrases, prepositional phrases) • Use these to provide details about a familiar or <u>new activity</u> or process (e.g. time, manner, place, cause) (e.g. They worked quietly; They ran across the soccer field.)	• Expand sentences with adverbials (e.g. adverbs, adverb phrases, prepositional phrases) • Use these to provide details about a <u>range</u> of familiar and new activities or processes.(e.g. time, manner, place, cause) (e.g. They worked quietly all night in their room.)
GRADE 4		
• Expand sentences with familiar adverbials (e.g. basic prepositional phrases) • Use these to provide details about a familiar activity or process (e.g. time, manner, place, cause) (e.g. They walked to the soccer field.)	• Expand sentences with a <u>growing variety</u> of adverbials (e.g. adverbs, prepositional phrases) • Use these to provide details about a familiar or <u>new activity</u> or process (e.g. time, manner, place, cause) (e.g. They worked quietly; They ran across the soccer field.)	• Expand sentences with a <u>variety</u> of adverbials (e.g. adverbs, adverb phrases, prepositional phrases) • Use these to provide details about a <u>variety</u> of familiar and new activities or processes.(e.g. time, manner, place, cause) (e.g. They worked quietly all night in their room.)
GRADE 5		
• Expand and enrich sentences with adverbials (e.g. adverbs, adverb phrases, prepositional phrases) • Use these to provide details about a familiar activity or process (e.g. time, manner, place, cause)	• Expand and enrich sentences with adverbials (e.g. adverbs, adverb phrases, prepositional phrases) • Use these to provide details about a familiar or <u>new activity</u> or process (e.g. time, manner, place, cause)	• Expand and enrich sentences with adverbials (e.g. adverbs, adverb phrases, prepositional phrases) • Use these to provide details about a <u>variety</u> of familiar and new activities or processes.(e.g. time, manner, place, cause)

Writing: *Justify an Opinion*

ELD Standards Record Sheet

CA ELD Standards & Proficiency Levels
Part II: Learning About How English Works
C.6 Connecting Ideas

EMERGING (EM) →	EXPANDING (EX) →	BRIDGING (BR)
Requires **Substantial** Support	Requires **Moderate** Support	Requires **Light** Support
GRADE 3		

• Combine clauses in a few basic ways
• To make connections between and to join ideas (e.g. creating compound sentences using and, but, so)
	• Combine clauses in an <u>increasing variety</u> of ways (e.g. creating compound and complex sentences)
	• to make connections between and to join ideas, for example:
	  ◦ <u>to express cause/effect (e.g. The deer ran because the mountain lion came.)</u>
	  ◦ <u>to make a concession (e.g. She studied all night even though she wasn't feeling well.)</u>
		• Combine clauses in a <u>wide variety</u> of ways (e.g. creating compound and complex sentences)
		• to make connections between and to join ideas, for example:
		  ◦ to express cause/effect (e.g. The deer ran because the mountain lion approached them.)
		  ◦ to make a concession(e.g. She studied all night even though she wasn't feeling well.)
		  ◦ <u>to link two ideas that happen at the same time (e.g. The cubs played while their mother hunted.)</u>

GRADE 4		

• Combine clauses in a few basic ways
• To make connections between and to join ideas in sentences (e.g. creating compound sentences using coordinate conjunctions, such as and, but, so)
	• Combine clauses in an <u>increasing variety</u> of ways (e.g. creating complex sentences using familiar subordinate conjunctions)
	• to make connections between and to join ideas in sentences, for example:
	  ◦ <u>to express cause/effect (e.g. The deer ran because the mountain lion came.)</u>
	  ◦ <u>to make a concession (e.g. She studied all night even though she wasn't feeling well.)</u>
		• Combine clauses in a <u>wide variety</u> of ways (e.g. creating complex sentences using a variety of subordinate conjunctions)
		• to make connections between and to join ideas, for example:
		  ◦ to express cause/effect (e.g. Since the lion was at the waterhole, the deer ran away.)
		  ◦ to make a concession
		  ◦ <u>to link two ideas that happen at the same time (e.g. The cubs played while their mother hunted.)</u>

GRADE 5		

• Combine clauses in a few basic ways
• To make connections between and to join ideas
• To provide evidence to support ideas or opinions (e.g. You must X because X.) (e.g. creating compound sentences using and, but, so)
	• Combine clauses in an <u>increasing variety</u> of ways (e.g. creating compound and complex sentences)
	• to make connections between and to join ideas, for example:
	  ◦ <u>to express cause/effect (e.g. The deer ran because the mountain lion came.)</u>
	  ◦ <u>to make a concession(e.g. She studied all night even though she wasn't feeling well.)</u>
	• To provide reasons to support ideas (e.g. X is an extremely good book because X)
		• Combine clauses in a <u>wide variety</u> of ways (e.g. creating compound and complex sentences)
		• to make connections between and to join ideas, for example:
		  ◦ to express cause/effect (e.g. The deer ran because the mountain lion approached them.)
		  ◦ to make a concession (e.g. She studied all night even though she wasn't feeling well.)
		  ◦ <u>to link two ideas that happen at the same time (e.g. The cubs played while their mother hunted.)</u>
		• To provide reasons to support ideas (e.g The author persuades the reader by X.)

122

Writing: *Justify an Opinion*

ELD Standards Record Sheet

Teacher: _____ **Class:** _____

Standards: *PI.C.11*

Guided Activities and Proficiency Levels:

Students:	#1	#2	#3	#4	#5
	EM / EX / BR	EM / EX / BR	EM / EX / BR	EM / EX / BR	EM / EX / BR
	EM / EX / BR	EM / EX / BR	EM / EX / BR	EM / EX / BR	EM / EX / BR
	EM / EX / BR	EM / EX / BR	EM / EX / BR	EM / EX / BR	EM / EX / BR
	EM / EX / BR	EM / EX / BR	EM / EX / BR	EM / EX / BR	EM / EX / BR
	EM / EX / BR	EM / EX / BR	EM / EX / BR	EM / EX / BR	EM / EX / BR
	EM / EX / BR	EM / EX / BR	EM / EX / BR	EM / EX / BR	EM / EX / BR
	EM / EX / BR	EM / EX / BR	EM / EX / BR	EM / EX / BR	EM / EX / BR
	EM / EX / BR	EM / EX / BR	EM / EX / BR	EM / EX / BR	EM / EX / BR
	EM / EX / BR	EM / EX / BR	EM / EX / BR	EM / EX / BR	EM / EX / BR
	EM / EX / BR	EM / EX / BR	EM / EX / BR	EM / EX / BR	EM / EX / BR
	EM / EX / BR	EM / EX / BR	EM / EX / BR	EM / EX / BR	EM / EX / BR
	EM / EX / BR	EM / EX / BR	EM / EX / BR	EM / EX / BR	EM / EX / BR
	EM / EX / BR	EM / EX / BR	EM / EX / BR	EM / EX / BR	EM / EX / BR
	EM / EX / BR	EM / EX / BR	EM / EX / BR	EM / EX / BR	EM / EX / BR
	EM / EX / BR	EM / EX / BR	EM / EX / BR	EM / EX / BR	EM / EX / BR
	EM / EX / BR	EM / EX / BR	EM / EX / BR	EM / EX / BR	EM / EX / BR
	EM / EX / BR	EM / EX / BR	EM / EX / BR	EM / EX / BR	EM / EX / BR
	EM / EX / BR	EM / EX / BR	EM / EX / BR	EM / EX / BR	EM / EX / BR
	EM / EX / BR	EM / EX / BR	EM / EX / BR	EM / EX / BR	EM / EX / BR
	EM / EX / BR	EM / EX / BR	EM / EX / BR	EM / EX / BR	EM / EX / BR

ELD Standards Record Sheet

Teacher: _____ **Class:** _____

Standards: *PI.C.12*   **Guided Activities and Proficiency Levels:**

Students:	#1	#2	#3	#4	#5
	EM / EX / BR	EM / EX / BR	EM / EX / BR	EM / EX / BR	EM / EX / BR
	EM / EX / BR	EM / EX / BR	EM / EX / BR	EM / EX / BR	EM / EX / BR
	EM / EX / BR	EM / EX / BR	EM / EX / BR	EM / EX / BR	EM / EX / BR
	EM / EX / BR	EM / EX / BR	EM / EX / BR	EM / EX / BR	EM / EX / BR
	EM / EX / BR	EM / EX / BR	EM / EX / BR	EM / EX / BR	EM / EX / BR
	EM / EX / BR	EM / EX / BR	EM / EX / BR	EM / EX / BR	EM / EX / BR
	EM / EX / BR	EM / EX / BR	EM / EX / BR	EM / EX / BR	EM / EX / BR
	EM / EX / BR	EM / EX / BR	EM / EX / BR	EM / EX / BR	EM / EX / BR
	EM / EX / BR	EM / EX / BR	EM / EX / BR	EM / EX / BR	EM / EX / BR
	EM / EX / BR	EM / EX / BR	EM / EX / BR	EM / EX / BR	EM / EX / BR
	EM / EX / BR	EM / EX / BR	EM / EX / BR	EM / EX / BR	EM / EX / BR
	EM / EX / BR	EM / EX / BR	EM / EX / BR	EM / EX / BR	EM / EX / BR
	EM / EX / BR	EM / EX / BR	EM / EX / BR	EM / EX / BR	EM / EX / BR
	EM / EX / BR	EM / EX / BR	EM / EX / BR	EM / EX / BR	EM / EX / BR
	EM / EX / BR	EM / EX / BR	EM / EX / BR	EM / EX / BR	EM / EX / BR
	EM / EX / BR	EM / EX / BR	EM / EX / BR	EM / EX / BR	EM / EX / BR
	EM / EX / BR	EM / EX / BR	EM / EX / BR	EM / EX / BR	EM / EX / BR
	EM / EX / BR	EM / EX / BR	EM / EX / BR	EM / EX / BR	EM / EX / BR
	EM / EX / BR	EM / EX / BR	EM / EX / BR	EM / EX / BR	EM / EX / BR

ELD Standards Record Sheet

Teacher: _____ **Class:** _____

Standards: *PII.A.1*

Guided Activities and Proficiency Levels:

Students:	#1	#2	#3	#4	#5
	EM / EX / BR	EM / EX / BR	EM / EX / BR	EM / EX / BR	EM / EX / BR
	EM / EX / BR	EM / EX / BR	EM / EX / BR	EM / EX / BR	EM / EX / BR
	EM / EX / BR	EM / EX / BR	EM / EX / BR	EM / EX / BR	EM / EX / BR
	EM / EX / BR	EM / EX / BR	EM / EX / BR	EM / EX / BR	EM / EX / BR
	EM / EX / BR	EM / EX / BR	EM / EX / BR	EM / EX / BR	EM / EX / BR
	EM / EX / BR	EM / EX / BR	EM / EX / BR	EM / EX / BR	EM / EX / BR
	EM / EX / BR	EM / EX / BR	EM / EX / BR	EM / EX / BR	EM / EX / BR
	EM / EX / BR	EM / EX / BR	EM / EX / BR	EM / EX / BR	EM / EX / BR
	EM / EX / BR	EM / EX / BR	EM / EX / BR	EM / EX / BR	EM / EX / BR
	EM / EX / BR	EM / EX / BR	EM / EX / BR	EM / EX / BR	EM / EX / BR
	EM / EX / BR	EM / EX / BR	EM / EX / BR	EM / EX / BR	EM / EX / BR
	EM / EX / BR	EM / EX / BR	EM / EX / BR	EM / EX / BR	EM / EX / BR
	EM / EX / BR	EM / EX / BR	EM / EX / BR	EM / EX / BR	EM / EX / BR
	EM / EX / BR	EM / EX / BR	EM / EX / BR	EM / EX / BR	EM / EX / BR
	EM / EX / BR	EM / EX / BR	EM / EX / BR	EM / EX / BR	EM / EX / BR
	EM / EX / BR	EM / EX / BR	EM / EX / BR	EM / EX / BR	EM / EX / BR
	EM / EX / BR	EM / EX / BR	EM / EX / BR	EM / EX / BR	EM / EX / BR
	EM / EX / BR	EM / EX / BR	EM / EX / BR	EM / EX / BR	EM / EX / BR
	EM / EX / BR	EM / EX / BR	EM / EX / BR	EM / EX / BR	EM / EX / BR

Writing: *Justify an Opinion*

ELD Standards Record Sheet

Teacher: _____ **Class:** _____

Standards: *PII.B.3*

Guided Activities and Proficiency Levels:

Students:	#1	#2	#3	#4	#5
	EM / EX / BR	EM / EX / BR	EM / EX / BR	EM / EX / BR	EM / EX / BR
	EM / EX / BR	EM / EX / BR	EM / EX / BR	EM / EX / BR	EM / EX / BR
	EM / EX / BR	EM / EX / BR	EM / EX / BR	EM / EX / BR	EM / EX / BR
	EM / EX / BR	EM / EX / BR	EM / EX / BR	EM / EX / BR	EM / EX / BR
	EM / EX / BR	EM / EX / BR	EM / EX / BR	EM / EX / BR	EM / EX / BR
	EM / EX / BR	EM / EX / BR	EM / EX / BR	EM / EX / BR	EM / EX / BR
	EM / EX / BR	EM / EX / BR	EM / EX / BR	EM / EX / BR	EM / EX / BR
	EM / EX / BR	EM / EX / BR	EM / EX / BR	EM / EX / BR	EM / EX / BR
	EM / EX / BR	EM / EX / BR	EM / EX / BR	EM / EX / BR	EM / EX / BR
	EM / EX / BR	EM / EX / BR	EM / EX / BR	EM / EX / BR	EM / EX / BR
	EM / EX / BR	EM / EX / BR	EM / EX / BR	EM / EX / BR	EM / EX / BR
	EM / EX / BR	EM / EX / BR	EM / EX / BR	EM / EX / BR	EM / EX / BR
	EM / EX / BR	EM / EX / BR	EM / EX / BR	EM / EX / BR	EM / EX / BR
	EM / EX / BR	EM / EX / BR	EM / EX / BR	EM / EX / BR	EM / EX / BR
	EM / EX / BR	EM / EX / BR	EM / EX / BR	EM / EX / BR	EM / EX / BR
	EM / EX / BR	EM / EX / BR	EM / EX / BR	EM / EX / BR	EM / EX / BR
	EM / EX / BR	EM / EX / BR	EM / EX / BR	EM / EX / BR	EM / EX / BR
	EM / EX / BR	EM / EX / BR	EM / EX / BR	EM / EX / BR	EM / EX / BR
	EM / EX / BR	EM / EX / BR	EM / EX / BR	EM / EX / BR	EM / EX / BR
	EM / EX / BR	EM / EX / BR	EM / EX / BR	EM / EX / BR	EM / EX / BR

ELD Standards Record Sheet

Teacher: _____ **Class:** _____

Standards: *PII.B.4*

Guided Activities and Proficiency Levels:

Students:	#1	#2	#3	#4	#5
	EM / EX / BR	EM / EX / BR	EM / EX / BR	EM / EX / BR	EM / EX / BR
	EM / EX / BR	EM / EX / BR	EM / EX / BR	EM / EX / BR	EM / EX / BR
	EM / EX / BR	EM / EX / BR	EM / EX / BR	EM / EX / BR	EM / EX / BR
	EM / EX / BR	EM / EX / BR	EM / EX / BR	EM / EX / BR	EM / EX / BR
	EM / EX / BR	EM / EX / BR	EM / EX / BR	EM / EX / BR	EM / EX / BR
	EM / EX / BR	EM / EX / BR	EM / EX / BR	EM / EX / BR	EM / EX / BR
	EM / EX / BR	EM / EX / BR	EM / EX / BR	EM / EX / BR	EM / EX / BR
	EM / EX / BR	EM / EX / BR	EM / EX / BR	EM / EX / BR	EM / EX / BR
	EM / EX / BR	EM / EX / BR	EM / EX / BR	EM / EX / BR	EM / EX / BR
	EM / EX / BR	EM / EX / BR	EM / EX / BR	EM / EX / BR	EM / EX / BR
	EM / EX / BR	EM / EX / BR	EM / EX / BR	EM / EX / BR	EM / EX / BR
	EM / EX / BR	EM / EX / BR	EM / EX / BR	EM / EX / BR	EM / EX / BR
	EM / EX / BR	EM / EX / BR	EM / EX / BR	EM / EX / BR	EM / EX / BR
	EM / EX / BR	EM / EX / BR	EM / EX / BR	EM / EX / BR	EM / EX / BR
	EM / EX / BR	EM / EX / BR	EM / EX / BR	EM / EX / BR	EM / EX / BR
	EM / EX / BR	EM / EX / BR	EM / EX / BR	EM / EX / BR	EM / EX / BR
	EM / EX / BR	EM / EX / BR	EM / EX / BR	EM / EX / BR	EM / EX / BR
	EM / EX / BR	EM / EX / BR	EM / EX / BR	EM / EX / BR	EM / EX / BR
	EM / EX / BR	EM / EX / BR	EM / EX / BR	EM / EX / BR	EM / EX / BR
	EM / EX / BR	EM / EX / BR	EM / EX / BR	EM / EX / BR	EM / EX / BR

Writing: *Justify an Opinion*

ELD Standards Record Sheet

Teacher: _____ **Class:** _____

Standards: *PII.B.5*

Guided Activities and Proficiency Levels:

Students:	#1	#2	#3	#4	#5
	EM / EX / BR	EM / EX / BR	EM / EX / BR	EM / EX / BR	EM / EX / BR
	EM / EX / BR	EM / EX / BR	EM / EX / BR	EM / EX / BR	EM / EX / BR
	EM / EX / BR	EM / EX / BR	EM / EX / BR	EM / EX / BR	EM / EX / BR
	EM / EX / BR	EM / EX / BR	EM / EX / BR	EM / EX / BR	EM / EX / BR
	EM / EX / BR	EM / EX / BR	EM / EX / BR	EM / EX / BR	EM / EX / BR
	EM / EX / BR	EM / EX / BR	EM / EX / BR	EM / EX / BR	EM / EX / BR
	EM / EX / BR	EM / EX / BR	EM / EX / BR	EM / EX / BR	EM / EX / BR
	EM / EX / BR	EM / EX / BR	EM / EX / BR	EM / EX / BR	EM / EX / BR
	EM / EX / BR	EM / EX / BR	EM / EX / BR	EM / EX / BR	EM / EX / BR
	EM / EX / BR	EM / EX / BR	EM / EX / BR	EM / EX / BR	EM / EX / BR
	EM / EX / BR	EM / EX / BR	EM / EX / BR	EM / EX / BR	EM / EX / BR
	EM / EX / BR	EM / EX / BR	EM / EX / BR	EM / EX / BR	EM / EX / BR
	EM / EX / BR	EM / EX / BR	EM / EX / BR	EM / EX / BR	EM / EX / BR
	EM / EX / BR	EM / EX / BR	EM / EX / BR	EM / EX / BR	EM / EX / BR
	EM / EX / BR	EM / EX / BR	EM / EX / BR	EM / EX / BR	EM / EX / BR
	EM / EX / BR	EM / EX / BR	EM / EX / BR	EM / EX / BR	EM / EX / BR
	EM / EX / BR	EM / EX / BR	EM / EX / BR	EM / EX / BR	EM / EX / BR
	EM / EX / BR	EM / EX / BR	EM / EX / BR	EM / EX / BR	EM / EX / BR
	EM / EX / BR	EM / EX / BR	EM / EX / BR	EM / EX / BR	EM / EX / BR

ELD Standards Record Sheet

Teacher: _____ **Class:** _____

Standards: *PII.C.6*

Guided Activities and Proficiency Levels:

Students:	#1	#2	#3	#4	#5
	EM / EX / BR	EM / EX / BR	EM / EX / BR	EM / EX / BR	EM / EX / BR
	EM / EX / BR	EM / EX / BR	EM / EX / BR	EM / EX / BR	EM / EX / BR
	EM / EX / BR	EM / EX / BR	EM / EX / BR	EM / EX / BR	EM / EX / BR
	EM / EX / BR	EM / EX / BR	EM / EX / BR	EM / EX / BR	EM / EX / BR
	EM / EX / BR	EM / EX / BR	EM / EX / BR	EM / EX / BR	EM / EX / BR
	EM / EX / BR	EM / EX / BR	EM / EX / BR	EM / EX / BR	EM / EX / BR
	EM / EX / BR	EM / EX / BR	EM / EX / BR	EM / EX / BR	EM / EX / BR
	EM / EX / BR	EM / EX / BR	EM / EX / BR	EM / EX / BR	EM / EX / BR
	EM / EX / BR	EM / EX / BR	EM / EX / BR	EM / EX / BR	EM / EX / BR
	EM / EX / BR	EM / EX / BR	EM / EX / BR	EM / EX / BR	EM / EX / BR
	EM / EX / BR	EM / EX / BR	EM / EX / BR	EM / EX / BR	EM / EX / BR
	EM / EX / BR	EM / EX / BR	EM / EX / BR	EM / EX / BR	EM / EX / BR
	EM / EX / BR	EM / EX / BR	EM / EX / BR	EM / EX / BR	EM / EX / BR
	EM / EX / BR	EM / EX / BR	EM / EX / BR	EM / EX / BR	EM / EX / BR
	EM / EX / BR	EM / EX / BR	EM / EX / BR	EM / EX / BR	EM / EX / BR
	EM / EX / BR	EM / EX / BR	EM / EX / BR	EM / EX / BR	EM / EX / BR
	EM / EX / BR	EM / EX / BR	EM / EX / BR	EM / EX / BR	EM / EX / BR
	EM / EX / BR	EM / EX / BR	EM / EX / BR	EM / EX / BR	EM / EX / BR
	EM / EX / BR	EM / EX / BR	EM / EX / BR	EM / EX / BR	EM / EX / BR

Writing Practice #1

Name: _____

Directions: Read the writing prompt. Complete the graphic organizer to help you organize your opinion writing. You can use the sentence starters to help you.

Writing Prompt: *The students in your school have voted to get rid of assigned play areas during recess. Do you think that it is a good idea for assigned play areas to be eliminated during recess?*

-- State your opinion --
In my opinion ... _____   _____

Provide a reason	**Explain your reason with details/example**
One reason is ... _____ _____ _____	*For example, ...* _____ _____ _____

Provide a reason	**Explain your reason with details/example**
Another reason is ... _____ _____ _____	*What I mean is ...* _____ _____ _____

Provide a reason	**Explain your reason with details/example**
Equally important is... _____ _____ _____	*To clarify ...* _____ _____ _____

-- Restate your opinion --
In conclusion ... _____   _____

Writing Practice #1 - cont'd

Name:

Directions: Write your essay in the box below. Use the information in the graphic organizer. Remember to check your writing for grammar, capital letters, punctuation, and spelling.

Writing Prompt: *The students in your school have voted to get rid of assigned play areas during recess. Do you think that it is a good idea for assigned play areas to be eliminated during recess?*

Writing Practice #2

Name: _____

Directions: Read the writing prompt. Complete the graphic organizer to help you organize your opinion writing. You can use the sentence starters to help you.

Writing Prompt: *The teachers in your school have decided to take away art time to make more time for reading and math. Do you think that it is a good idea for art time to be removed?*

-- State your opinion --

In my opinion ... _____

_____

_____

Provide a reason	**Explain your reason with details/example**
One reason is ..._____ _____ _____	For example, ... _____ _____ _____

Provide a reason	**Explain your reason with details/example**
Another reason is ... _____ _____ _____	What I mean is ..._____ _____ _____

Provide a reason	**Explain your reason with details/example**
Equally important is..._____ _____ _____	To clarify ... _____ _____ _____

-- Restate your opinion --

In conclusion ... _____

_____

_____

Writing Practice #2 - cont'd

Name:

Directions: Write your essay in the box below. Use the information in the graphic organizer. Remember to check your writing for grammar, capital letters, punctuation, and spelling.

Writing Prompt: *The teachers in your school have decided to take away art time to make more time for reading and math. Do you think that it is a good idea for art time to be removed?*

Writing Practice #3

Name: ....

Directions: Read the writing prompt. Complete the graphic organizer to help you organize your opinion writing. You can use the sentence starters to help you.

Writing Prompt: *The school board members in your school have voted to make the school day 30 minutes longer. Do you think that it is a good idea for the school day to be 30 minutes longer?*

-- State your opinion --

In my opinion ... _____

_____

Provide a reason	**Explain your reason with details/example**
One reason is ... _____	*For example, ...* _____

Provide a reason	**Explain your reason with details/example**
Another reason is ... _____	*What I mean is ...* _____

Provide a reason	**Explain your reason with details/example**
Equally important is... _____	*To clarify ...* _____

-- Restate your opinion --

In conclusion ... _____

_____

Writing Practice #3 - cont'd

Name:

Directions: Write your essay in the box below. Use the information in the graphic organizer. Remember to check your writing for grammar, capital letters, punctuation, and spelling.

Writing Prompt: *The school board members in your school have voted to make the school day 30 minutes longer. Do you think that it is a good idea for the school day to be 30 minutes longer?*

Writing Practice #4

Name: ....

Directions: Read the writing prompt. Complete the graphic organizer to help you organize your opinion writing. You can use the sentence starters to help you.

....

<u>Writing Prompt:</u> *The parent volunteers in your school have decided to remodel the teachers' lounge using money from the student funds. Do you think that it is a good idea for student funds be used to remodel the teachers' lounge?*

-- State your opinion --

In my opinion ... _____

_____

Provide a reason	⟫⟫ **Explain your reason with details/example**
*One reason is ...*_____	*For example, ...* _____
_____	_____
_____	_____

Provide a reason	⟫⟫ **Explain your reason with details/example**
*Another reason is ...*_____	*What I mean is ...* _____
_____	_____
_____	_____

Provide a reason	⟫⟫ **Explain your reason with details/example**
*Equally important is...*_____	*To clarify ...* _____
_____	_____
_____	_____

-- Restate your opinion --

In conclusion ... _____

_____

Writing Practice #4 - cont'd

Name:

Directions: Write your essay in the box below. Use the information in the graphic organizer. Remember to check your writing for grammar, capital letters, punctuation, and spelling.

Writing Prompt: *The parent volunteers in your school have decided to remodel the teachers' lounge using money from the student funds. Do you think that it is a good idea for student funds be used to remodel the teachers' lounge?*

Writing Practice #5

Name: _____

Directions: Read the writing prompt. Complete the graphic organizer to help you organize your opinion writing. You can use the sentence starters to help you.

Writing Prompt: *The school librarian in your school has decided to open the school library once a week to save money. Do you think that it is a good idea for the school library to be open only once a week to save money?*

-- State your opinion --

In my opinion ... _____
_____

Provide a reason	**Explain your reason with details/example**
One reason is ... _____	*For example, ...* _____

Provide a reason	**Explain your reason with details/example**
Another reason is ... _____	*What I mean is ...* _____

Provide a reason	**Explain your reason with details/example**
Equally important is... _____	*To clarify ...* _____

-- Restate your opinion --

In conclusion ... _____
_____

Writing Practice #5 - cont'd

Name:

Directions: Write your essay in the box below. Use the information in the graphic organizer. Remember to check your writing for grammar, capital letters, punctuation, and spelling.

Writing Prompt: *The school librarian in your school has decided to open the school library once a week to save money. Do you think that it is a good idea for the school library to be open only once a week to save money?*

Writing Practice - *Blank Template*

Name: _____

Directions: Read the writing prompt. Complete the graphic organizer to help you organize your opinion writing. You can use the sentence starters to help you.

Writing Prompt:

-- State your opinion --

In my opinion ... _____

_____

Provide a reason	⟫ **Explain your reason with details/example**
*One reason is ...*_____	*For example, ...* _____
_____	_____
_____	_____

Provide a reason	⟫ **Explain your reason with details/example**
*Another reason is ...*_____	*What I mean is ...*_____
_____	_____
_____	_____

Provide a reason	⟫ **Explain your reason with details/example**
*Equally important is...*_____	*To clarify ...*_____
_____	_____
_____	_____

-- Restate your opinion --

In conclusion ... _____

_____

Writing Practice - *Blank Template*

Name: _____

Directions: Write your essay in the box below. Use the information in the graphic organizer. Remember to check your writing for grammar, capital letters, punctuation, and spelling.

Writing Prompt:

THIS PAGE INTENTIONALLY LEFT BLANK

Made in the USA
Las Vegas, NV
14 December 2023

82863684R00083